ILLUSTRATED TALES OF SHROPSHIRE

David Paul

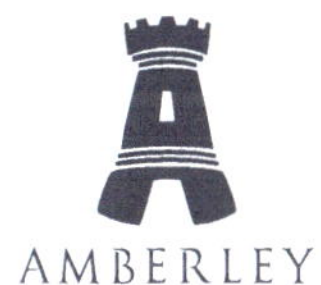

Acknowledgements

In conducting my research for this book, I have been able to draw heavily on the vast fund of collective knowledge that resides with library staff across the county, support for which I am most grateful. I would also wish to extend my thanks to the many people who made contributions, of any kind, with regard to the tales that I have been researching. In this context, I would wish to give my special thanks to Brian Hicks of Woolstaston for giving me a valuable insight into the tale of Revd Edmund Donald Carr and his heroic endeavours in ministering to his parishioners. I must also thank Peter Johnson for sharing his knowledge of the Battle of Maserfield, 5 August 641, and for his assistance in locating the site of St Oswald's Well. Similarly, I would wish to thank Grace Bennett of Church Stretton for relating many of the older and more traditional funeral customs as observed in Shropshire. I must also express my thanks to Mr Henry Thomas of Lakeside Classics for allowing me to use his excellent images of Bomere Pool, and also to Kari Hauge for directing me to Holy Trinity Church, Middleton-in-Chirbury. There are many other people to whom I owe a debt of thanks, but it would be remiss of me not to record my thanks to my wife, Janet, for accompanying me when taking photographs of the various locations mentioned in the text. I must also thank my son, Jon, who read and made a number of corrections to the manuscript. With reference to some of the black and white images included in the text, I would wish to state that despite prolonged and exhaustive enquiries, tracking down some copyright holders has not been possible. Finally, while I have tried to ensure that the information in the text is factually correct, any errors or inaccuracies are mine alone. The book does not purport, in any way, to be an academic text, but is aimed at the general reader.

First published 2019

Amberley Publishing
The Hill, Stroud
Gloucestershire, GL5 4EP

www.amberley-books.com

British Library Cataloguing in Publication Data.
A catalogue record for this book is available from the British Library.

ISBN 978 1 4456 9002 5 (paperback)
ISBN 978 1 4456 9003 2 (ebook)

Typesetting by Aura Technology and Software Services, India.
Printed in Great Britain.

Contents

Introduction

From its narrow, hedge-lined lanes to its modern, wide dual carriageways, Shropshire is a county as diverse as its roads would suggest. Righty famed for being the home of the Industrial Revolution, the county can also lay claim to having built the world's first iron-framed building, the Ditherington Flax Mill, which is now recognised as 'the grandfather of skyscrapers'. However, Shropshire also boasts, perhaps more than many other counties, a wealth of folklore, customs and tradition, from rope pulling – a re-enactment of the time when, during the siege of Ludlow by Henry VI, one of the town's bailiffs, a supporter of the king, was attempting to gain entrance to the town by opening Dinham Gate, dying in the attempt! – and the 'Maiden's Garland' hanging in the Church of St Calixtus in the hamlet of Astley Abbotts, which commemorates the untimely death of Hannah Phillips who drowned in the River Severn the day before her wedding, to the incredible tale of Charles II's escape from capture following his crushing defeat at the Battle of Worcester on 3 September 1651, when he was forced to seek shelter in an oak tree to save him from Cromwell's troops.

It is hoped that the stories that follow may preserve, in some small way, a few of the legends, traditions and folklore that help bestow upon Shropshire such a rich tradition and heritage.

David Paul

The Great Fire at Wem

Saturday 3 March 1677 is a day that will long be remembered in Wem, for it was on that day, between the hours of seven and eight o'clock, that a horrendous fire started. In a small house near the upper end of Leek Lane, a young girl, around fourteen years of age, was awaiting the return of her sister, Catharine Morris. Catherine had been washing linen at Oliver's Well. It is recorded that the young girl, Jane Churm, in order to have everything ready for her sister's return, went upstairs to fetch some fuel, which was kept under a bed, the idea being that she'd have a good fire burning when her sister returned. In the process of gathering kindling for the fire, Jane inadvertently dropped her candle, which caught the thatch and, in turn, set the house in flames. Unfortunately for Jane, there was a strong wind blowing that night, making it impossible to quench the blaze. To make matters worse, there had been very little rain, meaning that the nearby straw-covered houses were soon also being consumed by the flames. Before very long, most of the town was ablaze.

The strong easterly wind blew the burning thatch all over the place, and soon the flames were reaching as far as High Street, Cripple Street and the Horse Fair, consuming everything in their path as far as Burton's pit, save for the free school and the house of George Groom. The wind then changed direction to the south-west, taking the fire towards Noble Street as far as Drawwell House. By this time many people from outlying districts had come to give their assistance and offered to help Mr Higginson remove the contents of his property, but he would not hear of it, preferring instead to focus his efforts on the preservation

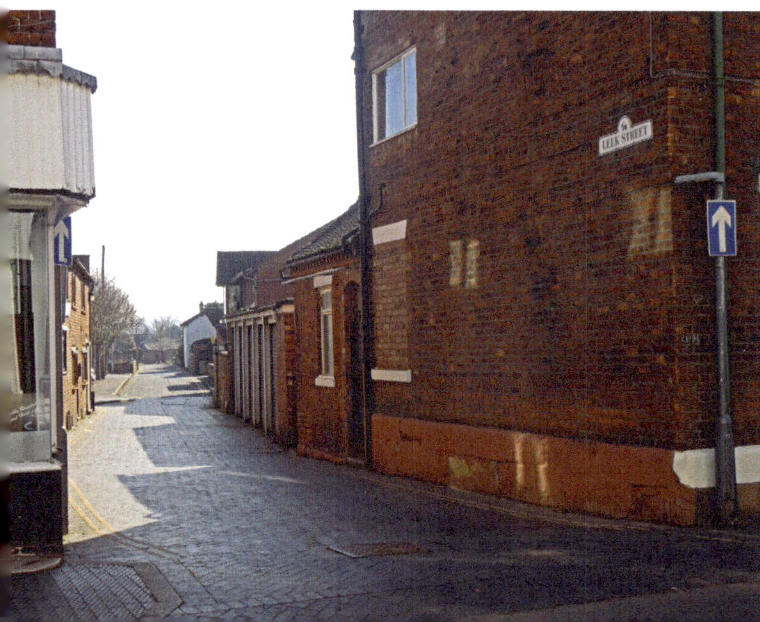

Leek Lane (Leek Street today), where the fire started.

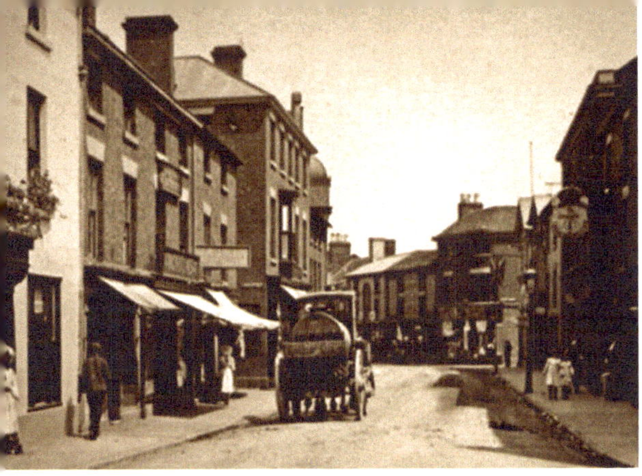

Above: Wem High Street during the nineteenth century.

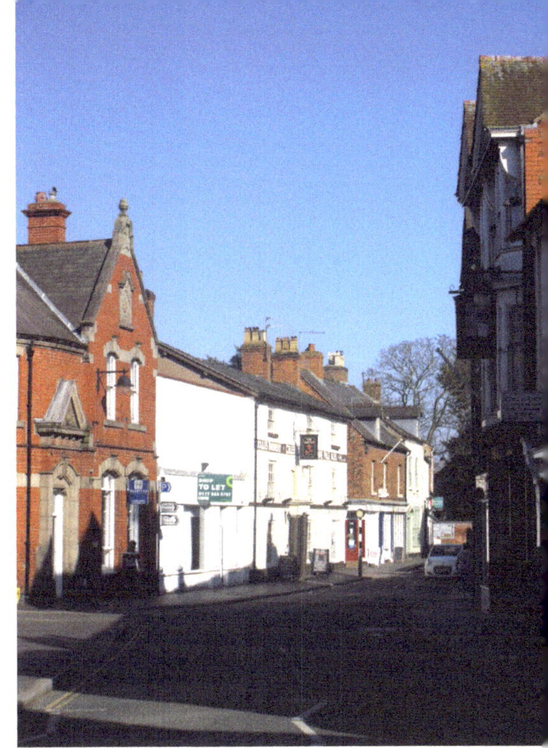

Right: Wem High Street today.

of his house. All of his barns and outbuildings were on fire, and the flames then spread to the house itself, but his neighbours doused the fire with untold buckets of water and the blaze was contained. However, the flames spread on the other side advancing eastwards along High Street. When the fire reached Mill Street, it consumed the rector's barns, and in Leek Lane it burned as far as William Smith's house. There was extensive damage to the church, the church steeple, the market house, in excess of 140 dwelling houses and an even larger number of outhouses. The devastation had been caused in less than an hour and, at its height, the blaze could be seen some 9 miles away, lighting up the countryside such that it was brighter than the light from the full moon.

There was much confusion, with people running in every direction, some away from the fire, while others endeavoured to save their houses or, failing that, to rescue as many of their most valuable effects. One man, Richard Sherratt, a shoemaker, was consumed in the flames together with several of his cattle. He'd gone into his shop to fetch a pair of shoes and was last seen walking by the market house, which then collapsed on him.

The cost of rebuilding was huge. An estimate was made of the cost to repair and rebuild all of the buildings that had been consumed, and this amounted to £14,760 10*s*. The estimation of the cost of replacing all of the household goods was £8,916 13*s* 1*d*.

Many are of the belief that, in her grief, the ghost of Jane Churm can still be seen wandering through the town hall.

Location: SY4 5EP

The Roaring Bull of Bagbury

In days now long passed, there lived a very nasty man at Bagbury Hall on the borders of Shropshire and Montgomery. It was reputed that during his life he had only ever done two good things: the first was to give a waistcoat to a poor old man, and the other was to give a piece of bread and cheese to a poor boy. He was so ashamed of his callous and selfish nature that just before he died, he confessed to all of his many shortcomings. Then, when he did die, his soul could not find rest and his ghost roamed through the house. The strange thing was, his ghost entered the house as a roaring bull, and he would stamp and roar until the boards and shutters of the house created such a cacophony that it became impossible for anyone to live anywhere near. It was said that in his wildest moments, even the tiles on the roof became dislodged and flew off in all directions. Fortunately, the bull never appeared until nine or ten at night, so he didn't cause that much trouble. As time went on, however, he became more wilful, and started to come out about seven or eight in the evening. This did cause some consternation to folk and they looked for ways of stopping his nightly rampage. Eventually, when all other avenues had been exhausted, they decided to call twelve parsons to exorcise his ghost.

Hyssington Primitive Methodist Chapel.

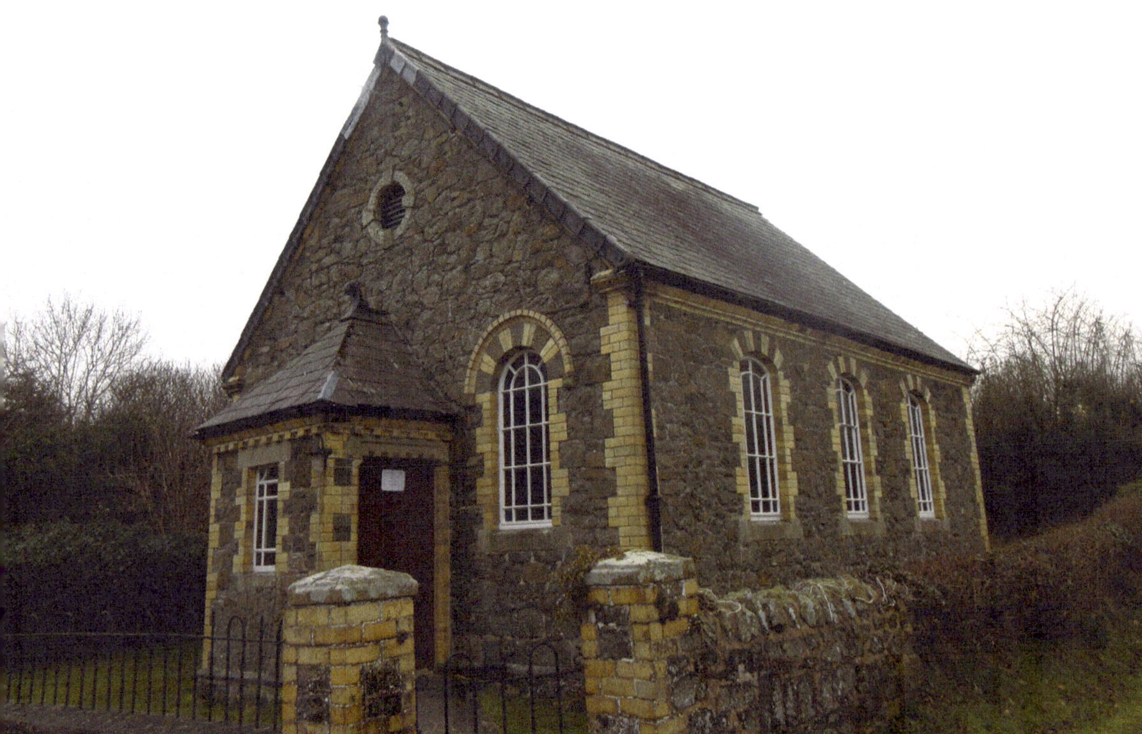

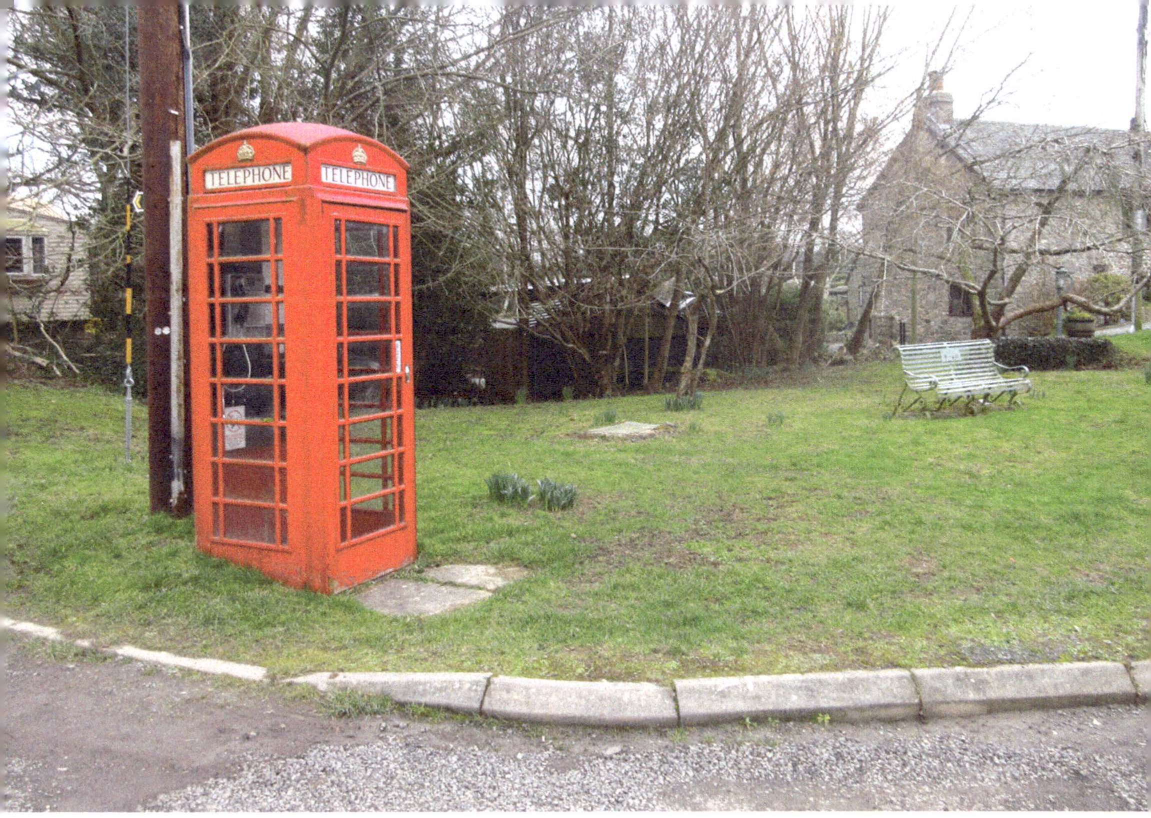

Village Green and telephone box.

The parsons did encounter some difficulty, but eventually the bull was taken to Hyssington church. The twelve parsons all held lighted candles, according to the ritual of the ceremony. However, one of the parsons, Parson Pigeon, who happened to be blind, knew the ways of the bull and knew that he would make a rush; he therefore decided to shelter his candle in his top boot. When the bull did make a great rush, as the blind parson had anticipated, all of the candles went out, save for his, and the bull, who had become comparatively small and tame, began to grow before their eyes, and charged towards the church wall, causing it to crack from top to bottom. Then, just in the nick of time, the parsons were able to get their candles relighted from Parson Pigeon's, and regained power over the bull whose power gradually diminished. They continued reading until the bull became so small that they were able to contain him in a snuff box. Continuing with his dialogue, the bull petitioned that he might be laid under Bagbury Bridge, so that he could cause every woman who passed over to lose her babe and every mare her foal. This request was not given any consideration by the assembled parsons, and he was condemned to be laid in the Red Sea for a thousand years.

There are, however, still some people living in the village who believe that the bull lies in an old shoe under the door stone of Hyssington church, while others pass over Bagbury Bridge with a degree of apprehension, or dread seeing apparitions in Bagbury Hall.

Location: SY15 6EQ

The White Lady of Longnor

Running alongside the road to Leebotwood is the Black Pool and, from time to time, the White Lady of Longnor emerges from the bottomless pool. One night the 'parson's man' at Longnor was walking over the narrow footbridge near to the ford over Longnor Brook when he saw a lady coming towards him.

> I sid 'er a-cummin',' he said, 'an' I thinks, 'ere's a nice young wench. Well, thinks I, who she be, I'll gi'e 'er a fright. I was a young fellow then, yo' known, an' I waited till 'er come close up to me, right i' the middle o' the bridge, an' I stretched out my arms, an' I clasped 'er in 'em tight, An' theer was nothin'.

The 'parson's man', having described her in great detail, then went on to say that he'd heard that she'd come along to attend the party and dance that was being held in the garden. Joe Wigley, who was playing the fiddle on that occasion, said

Longnor Hall.

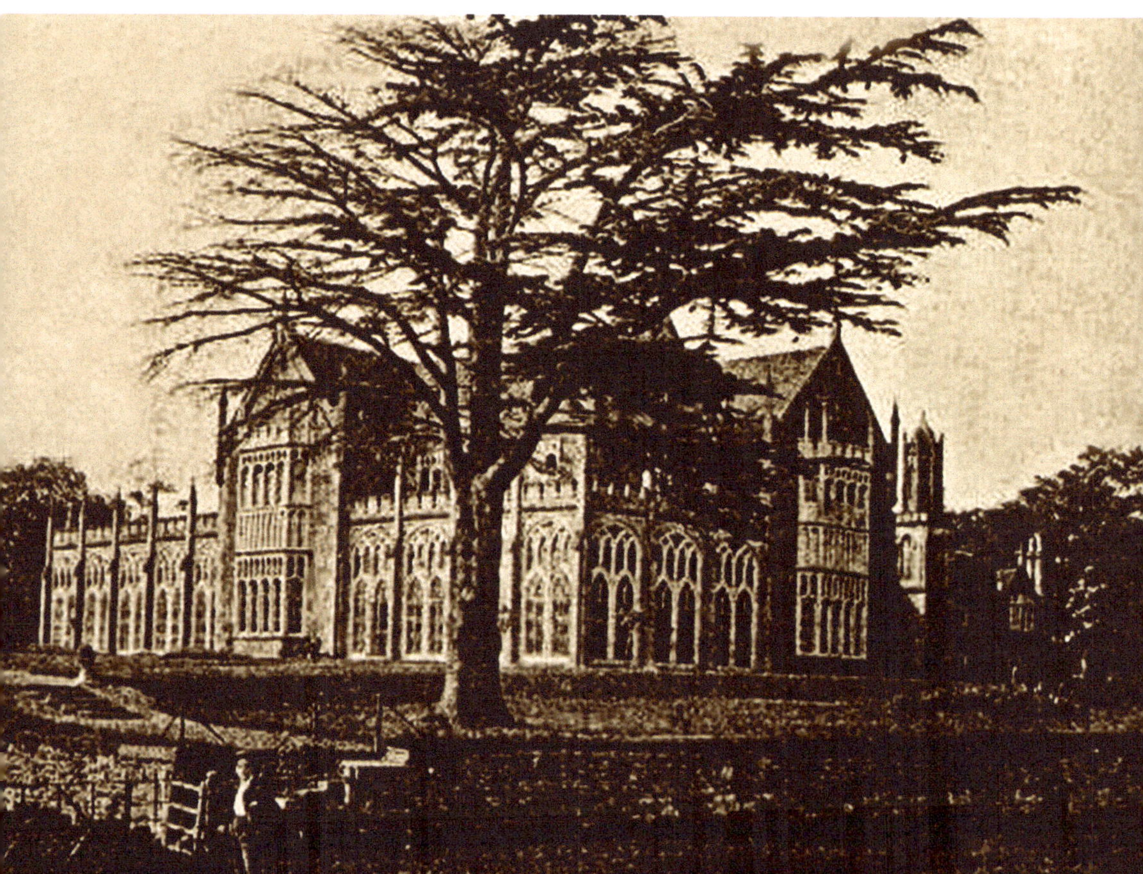

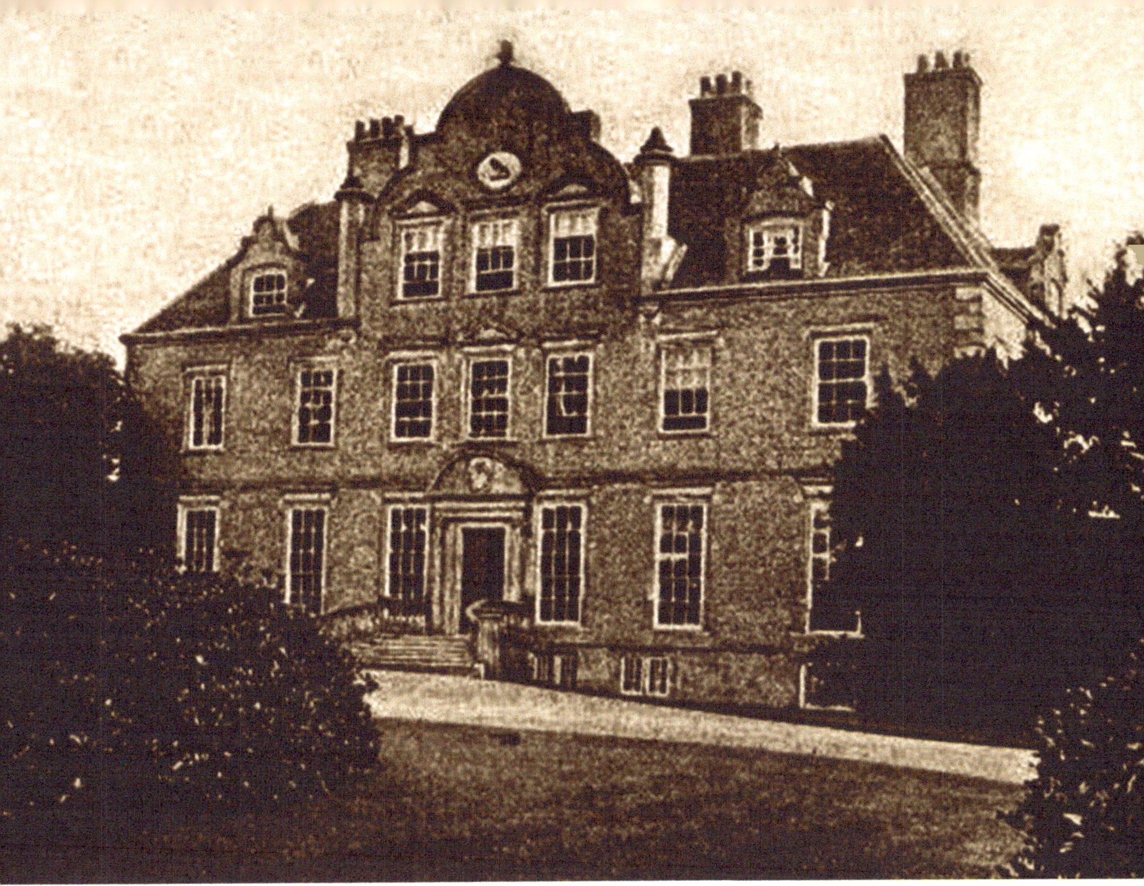

Early photograph of Longnor Hall.

that everyone was up dancing when all of a sudden she appeared and everyone at the party passed comment as to how beautiful she was dressed, as she was all in white. She danced around in the ring, but nobody could ever catch her so that they could dance with her alone. Then, after just a few dances, she was gone just as quickly as she had first appeared. It was only towards the end of the evening that rumour had it she was the White Lady. From that day onwards there was never any dancing in the garden of Longnor Hall.

Old Nancy, who was well known in the area, then related the story of the White Lady of Longnor, as many of the guests who were attending the party were not aware of the legend. She said that, even now, many years after the event that she was about to relate occurred, the White Lady is still reputed to haunt Longnor Hall. On the evening before her intended wedding a great ball was held at the hall. As the ball was reaching its end, the bride-to-be learnt that she had been jilted. On hearing this news she ran out into the grounds of the hall and threw herself in the Black Pool. Her body was never found. The story is still told that whenever there is a ball held at the hall she returns in search of an eligible partner. Unfortunately, whenever someone reaches out to dance with her, she disappears as quickly as she had appeared.

Location: SY4 4TG

Mitchell's Fold

On Stapeley Hill, which lies in the far west of the county, there stands a prehistoric stone circle that is known as Mitchell's Fold. Many years ago there was a great drought across the whole of the county of Shropshire. The drought was so prolonged that many of the county's wells dried up, crops in the fields died, as did farm livestock. Folk in the county became desperate, as they depended upon the crops and the farm animals to sustain their health and livelihoods. Recognising the desperate plight of the people, a kindly witch took pity on them and provided a magic cow, which she kept on Stapeley Hill. The cow itself was a beautiful large white cow and produced enough milk every day to supply every person living in the immediate area. The one stipulation was that anyone wanting milk could only bring one vessel to be filled, a rule which was strictly adhered to by everyone living in the village. However, as time went on, the good deed came to the notice of a malicious old witch, and she was determined to thwart the good witch's act of kindness. One night towards midnight, when nobody was around, the malicious old witch approached the cow that was standing alone on Stapeley Hill. Then, instead of a

Below left: Holy Trinity Church, Middleton-in-Chirbury.

Below right: Road leading from the village.

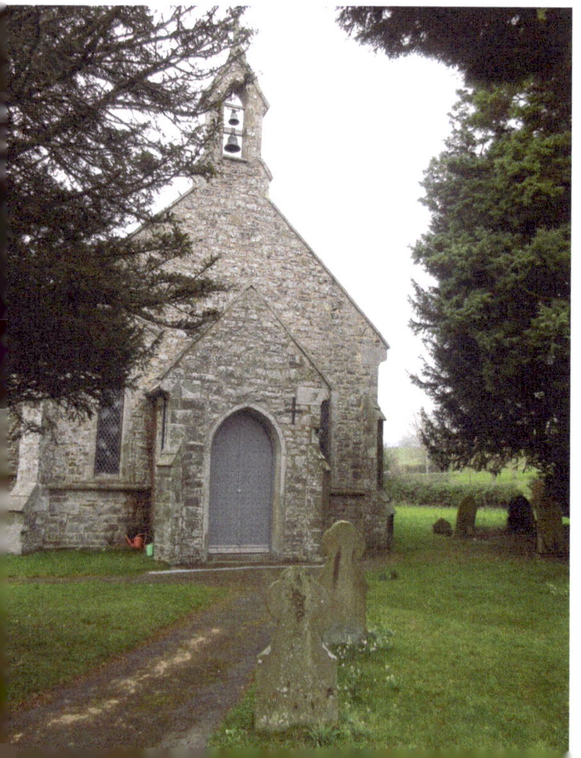

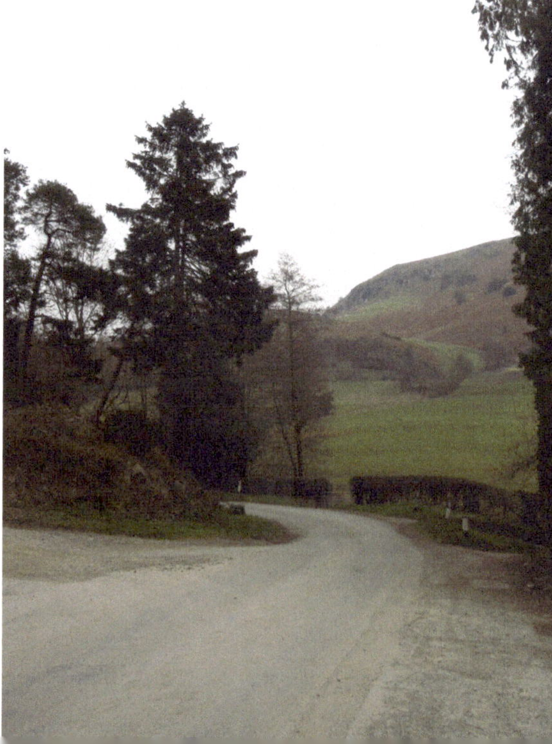

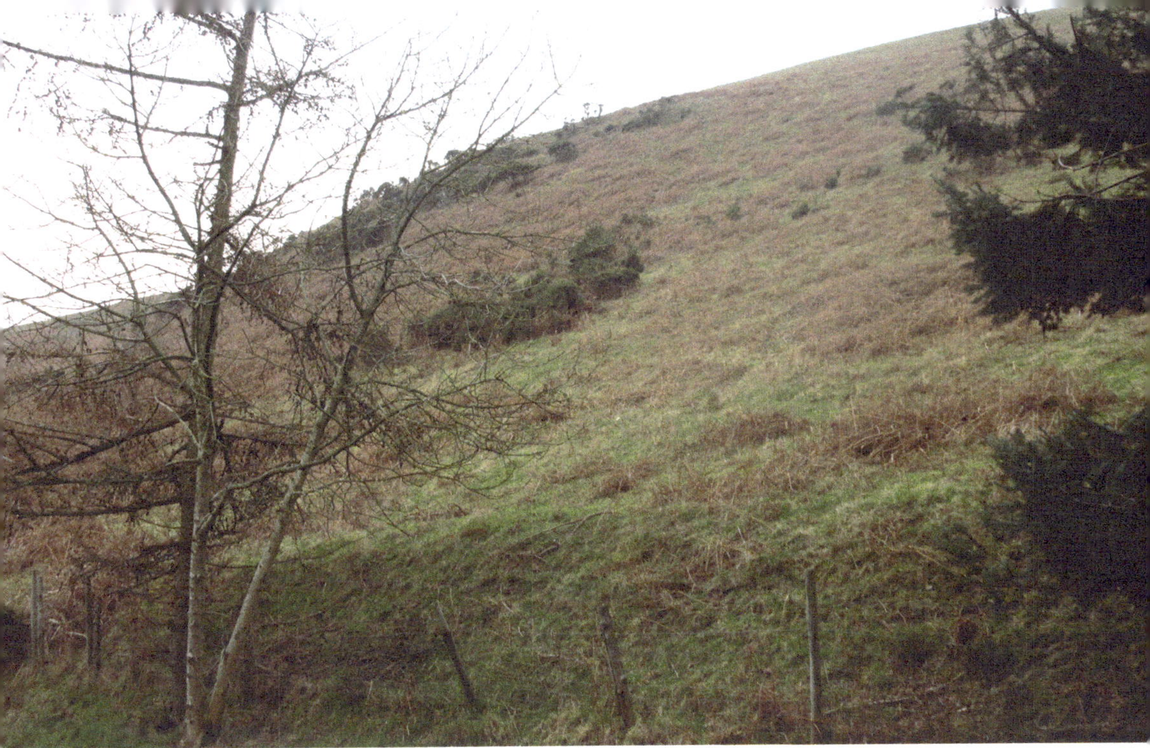

Stapeley Hill.

bucket, the witch placed a sieve-like riddle under the cow and started to milk her. The cow produced enough milk to fill a large bucket, but the witch went on milking. In fact, she milked it for so long that she completely exhausted what had, until now, been an apparently unending supply and the cow became totally confused as to what was going on. Just then a storm broke out on the other side of the hill and, by the light from the lightning flashes, the cow could see a large pool of wasted milk on the ground and realised immediately that she had been misled by the evil witch. She immediately fled madly from the hill and went into Warwickshire, where she became known as the celebrated Dun Cow of Warwick.

The following day when the village people arrived with their buckets for their daily milk, they found that the cow had gone. Unfortunately, this meant that these poor people who used to depend on her milk would be left to starve. They'd soon realised what had happened when they saw the pool of milk and the discarded sieve. They also saw that because of her malicious misdemeanour, the evil witch had been turned to stone. Straight away they placed another ring of stones around her petrified body just to ensure that she couldn't escape to perpetrate any more misdemeanours.

In 1879 a sandstone pillar was placed in Middleton Church, a church near to Stapeley Hill, recording the legend of the witch and the magic cow. It is more likely, however, that the stones were placed on Stapeley Hill by Bronze Age man more than 4,000 years ago.

The area became known as Mitchell's Fold because the witch's name was Mitchell.

Location: SY15 6DE

Ellesmere

There are many legends told about the great lake at Ellesmere, all of which have a common theme, that of punishment by flood being meted out because of some evil or wickedness being perpetrated.

It is believed that many years ago there was a vast swathe of meadowland where the lake now stands. Located in the middle of the meadows was a well from which everyone in the neighbourhood freely drew their water. Unfortunately, one day the farm and meadowland was sold to a new owner. He was a taciturn man who objected to village folk trampling over his land for their water. He stopped the tradition of everyone in the neighbourhood taking water from his well, and only allowed members of his own family to draw water from it. Then, just a few days after taking this decision, the farmer's wife went out with her bucket to get some water, but instead of seeing the well in the meadow, all she could see was a vast lake where the well had been located. The lake has remained there ever since, much to the annoyance of the farmer, as he had to continue to pay the same rent for the farm and the fields as a punishment for his uncharitable actions.

Another variation of the legend tells that many years ago it was difficult to draw clean water from any of the wells in the immediate vicinity, but there was a well in the middle of some of the meadowland that had the purest water to be found for miles around. Unfortunately, the farmer who owned the land where

Morning at Ellesmere.

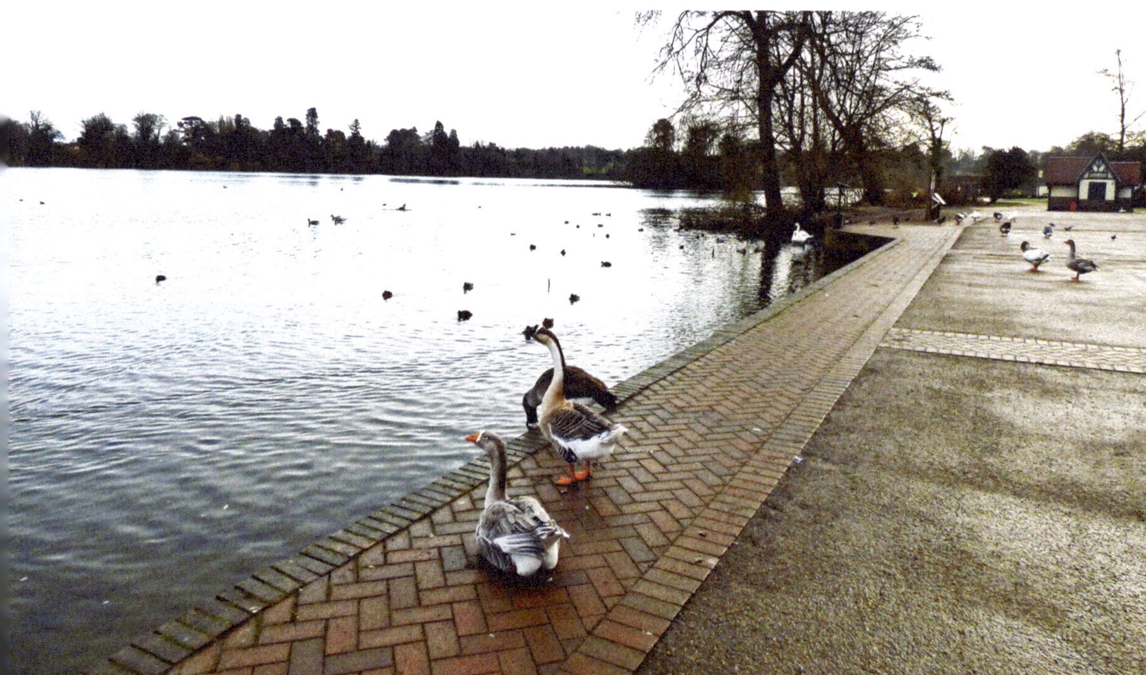

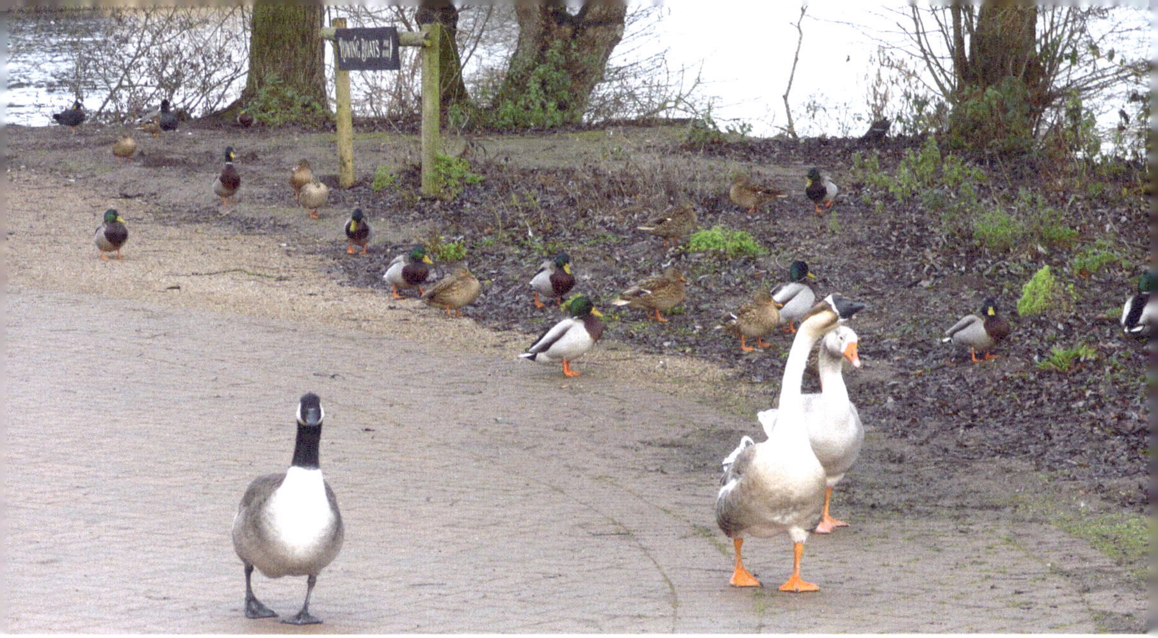

The birds at Ellesmere are totally oblivious of any legends.

the well was located insisted on charging a halfpenny for every bucketful that was taken. The people who were most affected were the poorer people in the neighbourhood. They prayed that something might be done to alleviate their desperate plight. Their prayers, in some way, were answered. One night the well burst, flooding all of the meadow. The lake that was created yielded plenty of water for all of the people in the parish.

A third version of the legend suggests that an old woman named Mrs Ellis once lived in a hamlet near to the farm. She had a pump in her yard that always gave the clearest water, but she would not sell or give any of it to her neighbours. However, as is often the way, one night the well overflowed. The following morning, neither Mrs Ellis nor her pump could be seen; the only sight was a vast lake that covered the whole of the area. Ever since that time, the lake has been known as 'Elles-mere.'

Location: SY12 0HD

The vast expanse of Ellesmere.

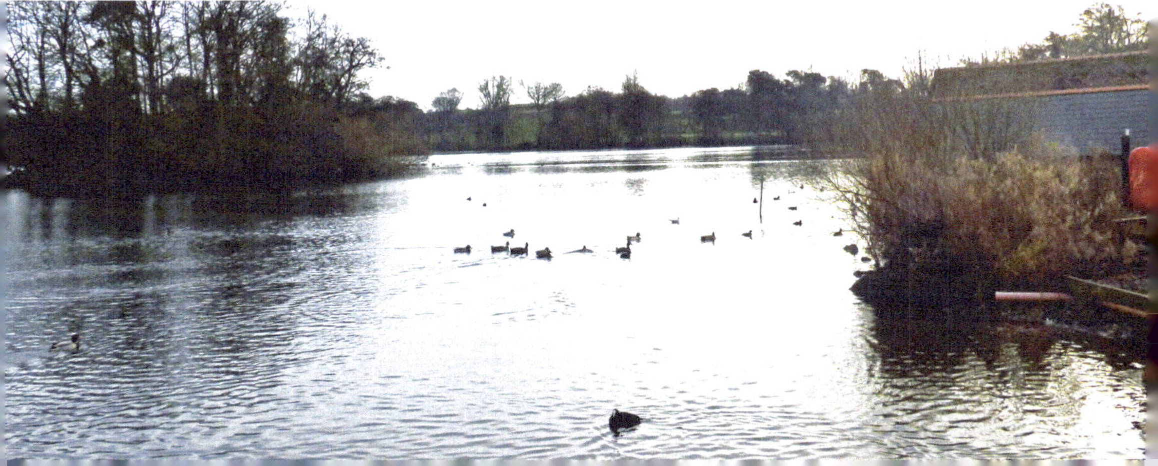

Wild Edric

After a day's hunting in the Forest of Clun, Wild Edric, one of Shropshire's most famous heroes, lost his way, and wandered aimlessly around until nightfall. By this time he was all alone save for his young page. Just as it was getting very dark, Edric saw the lights from a house shining in the distance. He turned and started to make his way towards the house. When he did eventually arrive at the house, he saw dancing in front of him a large group of gracious ladies, dressed in the finest linen dresses. He also noticed that all of the ladies were very beautiful, and all of them were much taller than most of the ladies that he was acquainted with. He thought that they might be elf maidens. In fact, it was Godda queen of the fairy folk dancing with her six sister fairies. As they were dancing around the vast hall, all of them were singing most melodiously, but Edric couldn't understand the words, as they were singing in a language that he'd never heard before. That confirmed, in his mind, that they were indeed fairy folk. One of the ladies was exceedingly beautiful, and Edric's heart was immediately filled with love for her. Totally beguiled and without any further thought or hesitation, Edric ran around the house looking for an entrance. Then, having found it, he ran straight in disturbing the gentile dancing, and snatched the maiden into his arms. The other dancers tried to restrain him, but he was too strong for them, and, assisted by his faithful page, he escaped, carrying with him the beautiful young maiden.

For the first three days while Edric was holding her against her will, Godda didn't utter a single word, but on the fourth day she made the following declaration:

> Good luck to you, my dear, and you will be lucky too, and enjoy health and peace and plenty, as long as you do not reproach me on account of my sisters, or the place from which you snatched me away, or anything connected with it. For on the day when you do so you will lose both your bride and your good fortune; and when I am taken away from you, you will pine away quickly to an early death.

This forthright statement totally confused Edric, but he pledged that he would be faithful and constant in his love for the queen of the fairies. A little while later they were married and Edric invited all of his noble friends from far and near to attend the festivities. News of the wedding soon reached the king, who invited the newly married couple to London where he was holding his court. When they arrived in London the king could not but gaze and admire the beauty of Edric's young wife. After being presented at court the couple left in order to return home. They continued to lead a very happy life until one evening Edric came home late from hunting and could not find his wife anywhere in their home. He was angry when she did finally appear and said, in no uncertain terms, 'I suppose it is your sisters who have detained you such a long time, have they not?'

As soon as Edric had mentioned Godda's sisters, she completely vanished. Edric was grief-stricken. He looked all over the place for her, and even went back to where he had first seen her all those years ago, but she was nowhere to be seen. His grief was all-consuming as he yearned to be reunited with her. Unable to continue without his dear wife by his side, Edric died of sorrow – a fate that she had foretold when he first fell in love with her.

Location: SY7 8QX

The Origin of the Wrekin

Somewhere lost in the mists of time there lived a wicked old giant in Wales. It was said that the giant, for some unknown reason, hated both the Mayor of Shrewsbury and all of the people who lived in the town. In fact, he hated them so much that he decided to make a dam across the River Severn that would cause a great flood, and, in doing so, would mean that the town would be completely deluged by the waters. So, having taken the trouble to dig a giant's spadeful of earth, he went on his way carrying the earth on his spade. Although he walked for several miles that day, he couldn't find his way to Shrewsbury. Goodness knows how he came to miss it, but miss it he did. He only realised his mistake as he was approaching Wellington. By this time, because of the heavy weight that he was carrying, he was running out of breath and energy, and wishing that his journey was at an end. After he'd been resting there for some time, he saw a cobbler approaching, carrying what looked like a sack of boots and shoes on his back. As it happens the cobbler, who lived in Wellington, was travelling back from Shrewsbury where he went every two weeks. When he went there he collected his customers' boots and shoes, which were in need of repair, and took them back to his workshop in Wellington.

The Wrekin from Cressage.

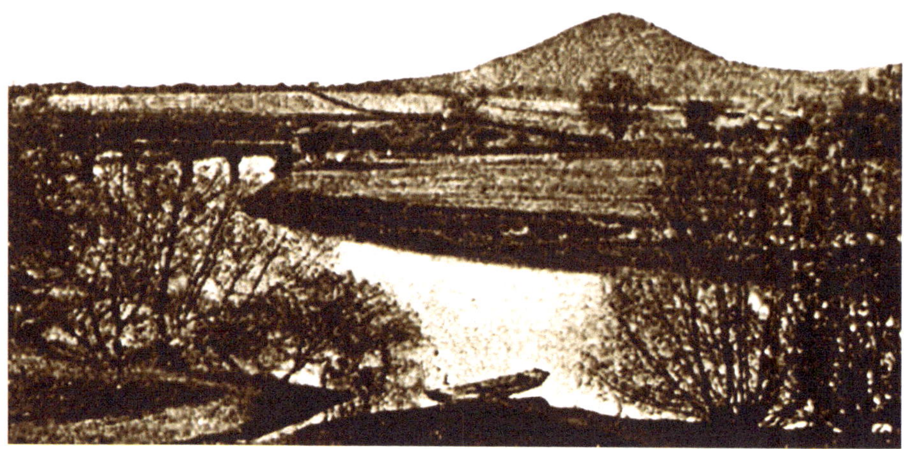

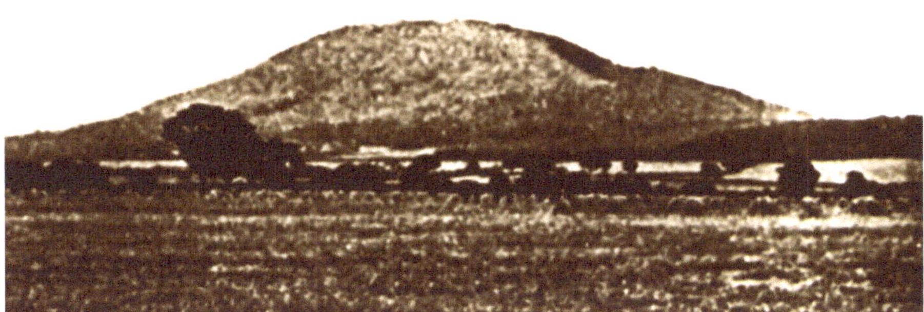

The Wrekin from the west.

As he approached, the giant called out, asking the cobbler how far it was to Shrewsbury. The cobbler replied, 'What do you want at Shrewsbury?' Without a moment's hesitation, the giant replied, 'To fill up the River Severn with this lump of earth I've got here. You will find this hard to believe, but I've an old grudge against the mayor and all of the people who live in Shrewsbury, and my one aim is to rid the earth of these people and their mayor.' The cobbler couldn't believe what he was hearing. Apart from anything else, if successful, it would mean that he would lose all of his customers. Thinking quickly, he spoke up: 'Well' said the cobbler, 'there's no way that you'll ever get to Shrewsbury; look at me. I've just come from there, and I've worn out all of these shoes and boots since I started on the road; look into my sack, and you'll get some idea of how far I've had to walk.'

Having looked into the sack on the cobbler's back, the giant sighed and then said. 'It's no use; I've already travelled a long way and I'm feeling tired and weary after such a long day. I don't think that I can go much further.' And with that he dropped all of the earth that he'd been carrying. Then, after he'd scraped his boots on his spade, he trudged off in a foul mood and made his way back to Wales and, from that day until this, he has never been seen or heard of again in Shropshire, but he did leave his mark on the local landscape. The Wrekin stands where he had dropped his load of earth and where he scraped off his boots became known as the Ercall.

Location: TF6 5AL

Shropshire Wedding Rituals

In and around the county of Shropshire there are still many rituals that are observed at traditional country weddings. A young bride about to dress and prepare for her wedding will first divest herself of all of her clothes before starting to attire herself in new and unwashed garments. There is, however, usually one exception to this ancient rule, and that is for the bride to wear something on her wedding day that has already been worn. Most ladies consider it to be a huge compliment to be asked to lend their wedding veils to friends for this purpose. It is often the case that the same lace veil has been worn in this way by a number of successive generations. Another ritual that is always meticulously observed is that the bride must never wear a green wedding dress. Even a green dress in a bride's trousseau is considered to bring bad luck. In former times, it was only brides of what may be considered to be the middle classes who aspired to wear a white wedding dress, whereas brides from the so-called lower or working classes tended to favour blue wedding dresses, hence the old English rhyme:

Something Olde,
Something New,
Something Borrowed,
Something Blue,
A Sixpence in your Shoe.

The rhyme lists four items that all brides should include somewhere in their wedding outfit or carry with her on her wedding day in order to bring her good luck. The sixpence was included to bring prosperity to the bride and her husband. Another custom decreed that if a younger sister should be married before her elder sibling, then the elder sister must dance at the wedding in her stocking feet. Similarly, the garters worn by the bride on her wedding day must have been bought by a close friend especially for the occasion. In return, it was customary for brides to give a sash and a pair of white gloves to her closest friends on her wedding day.

Many country folk insisted that in order to 'catch the infection of matrimony', bridesmaids should make it their business to brush against the bride.

It was recorded in 1829 at the wedding of Mrs Hare at Stoke-upon-Tern that as she walked through the churchyard, schoolchildren lined her path with garlands of flowers, and others walked before her strewing flowers. Also, neighbouring farmers fastened silver spoons, tankards and other ornaments onto each side the church gates. However, many of these more traditional wedding customs are dying out; it is now becoming more fashionable to throw handfuls of rice upon the newly married couple rather than flowers and flower petals.

The wedding ring itself is the centre of a number of superstitions. It is considered to be unlucky if the ring should fall to the ground before the marriage. Another commonly held superstition is that if either the bride or bridegroom should drop the ring during the wedding ceremony itself, then he or she will be the first of the couple to die.

Before setting off to the church, brides are cautioned that it is considered to be very unlucky for a wedding group to meet a funeral procession, so every effort must be made to avoid this situation.

Location: Throughout Shropshire.

The Pigotts of Chetwynd

Chetwynd is in the north-east of Shropshire, and there is a sad tale told concerning Madam Pigott, wife of the last of the Pigotts of Chetwynd. Madam Pigott's husband was desperate for an heir so that the line of Pigott would continue. There was elation when it became known that Madam Pigott was pregnant, but that joy soon turned to despondency when, during child birth, the doctor informed the soon-to-be father that mother and babe could not both survive. Faced with such a decision, the master instructed the doctor to 'lop the root to save the branch'. Somewhat disturbed by the harsh instruction, the doctor nevertheless obeyed. Madam Pigott was doomed to death before her time, which resulted in her spirit not being able to find any rest.

Unable to contain his grief and the misery that he had unwittingly inflicted on the household, Madam Pigott's husband went abroad. The house was shut up and the staff dismissed, save for the family of an old retainer who acted as caretakers.

After that time, Madam Pigott could often be seen either wandering in the gardens or through the hall itself. She was always dressed in a flowing white gown. When the caretaker's niece, who related the tale of Madam Pigott, saw the apparition, her aunt merely said, 'Never mind, child, it's only Madam Pigott. Put your apron over your head when she goes by, and she will do you no harm.'

Chetwynd Manor, immediately adjacent to St Michael and All Angels, Chetwynd.

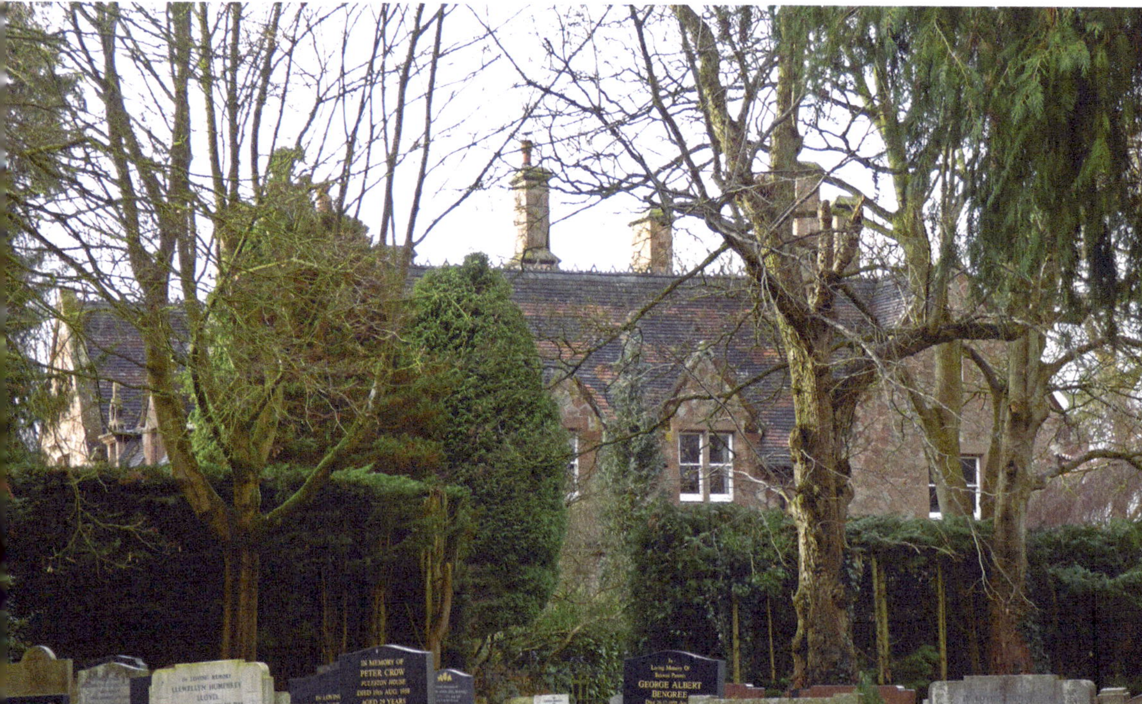

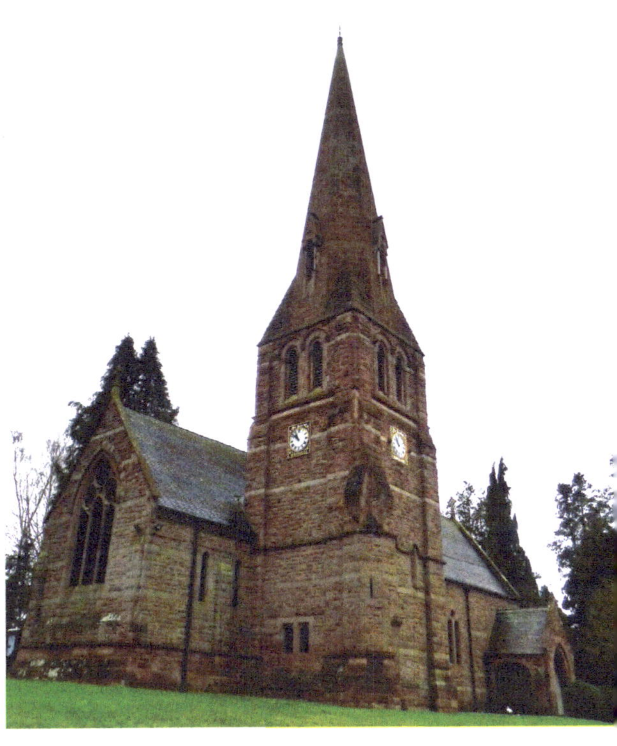
St Michael and All Angels, Chetwynd.

The stories relating to Madam Pigott's appearances were not always as innocuous as those related by the caretaker and her niece. Some suggested that Madam Pigott flew at midnight out of a trap door in the roof of the old Chetwynd Rectory and turned over a boulder in the lane between Chetwynd and Edgmond in the course of her nightly rambles, while others suggested that she was frequently seen on moonlit nights sitting on the wall of Chetwynd Park where it abuts on Cheney Hill, combing her baby's hair. The lane later became known as 'Madam Pigott's Hill', and the twisted tree root upon which she often sat was called 'Madam Pigott's armchair'. However, her exploits did not end there. It was reputed that whenever riders were off to fetch the doctor to assist at a birth, she would ride behind them until they reached running water, through which she could not pass.

It was with some reluctance, due to the sad circumstances of her demise, that the decision was taken to lay her ghost to rest. The time-honoured ritual was observed with twelve candles being lighted in the presence of twelve parsons praying and reading psalms. The ceremony continued until all of the candles save one went out. That candle belonged to Mr Foy, curate of Edgmond, whose honour it was to finally lay her to rest.

Some still hold to the view that she was first secured in a bottle, which was then thrown into Chetwynd Pool, but that the bottle was broken, and so the whole ceremony had to be repeated. When she was finally laid to rest, the neighbourhood once again had peace. However, even now, the oak tree at the foot of Chetwynd Scaur still quivers whenever Madam Pigott shakes it in her nightly wanderings, even though other trees in the vicinity are quite still.

Location: TF10 8EU

The Monster Fish of Bomere Pool

Some years ago now, a party of gentlemen, including the local squire, were fishing in Bomere Pool. The afternoon was passing in a very quiet and contented manner when, all of a sudden, an enormous fish was caught and hauled into the boat. There then followed much discussion and speculation as to the girth of the fish. Ultimately, because of its size, a bet was made that it had a larger girth than the squire himself, and that the squire's sword belt would not reach around the fish's waist. In order to test the validity of the bet, the squire unbuckled his belt, which was then fastened around the body of the fish, the task being completed with a degree of difficulty. As the buckling process was taking so long, the fish became impatient, and after wriggling free it was returned to his natural habitat, taking with him the squire's sword.

The Monster Fish of Bomere Pool still lives in the pool and is reputed to be bigger than any fish that ever swam. A sword is still worn at the fish's side, and no man can catch him. Many years ago there was an attempt to capture him, but it failed. A great net was brought, and, ultimately, the fish was entangled in

Bomere Pool.

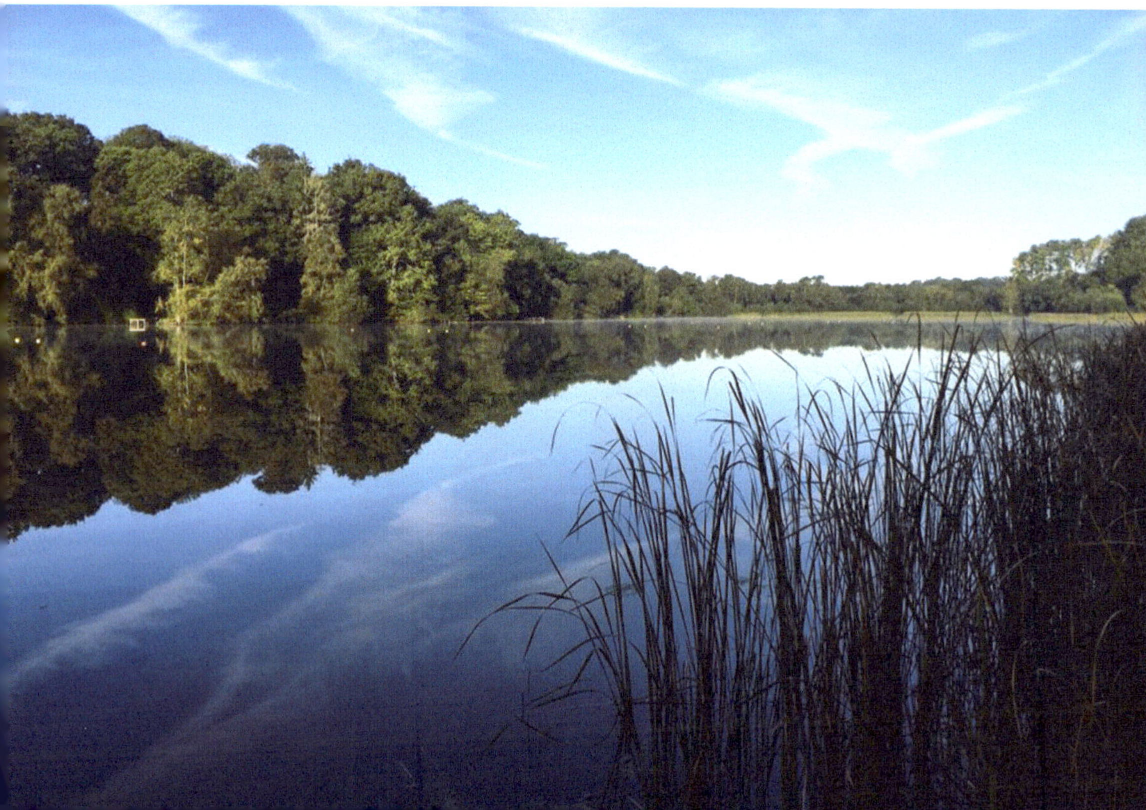

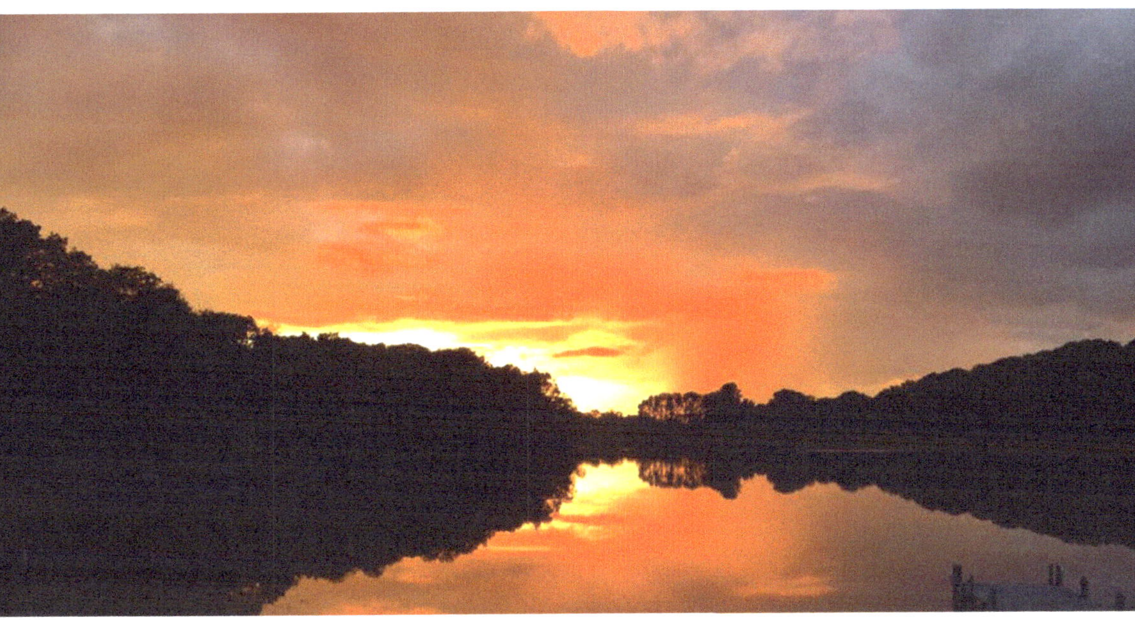

Early evening reflections on Bomere Pool.

it and brought nearly to the side. Just when the fishermen thought that they had won, the fish drew his sword, cut the net and escaped. Next, the fishermen made a net of iron links and managed to catch the giant fish in it. This time the fish was brought back to land, but somehow managed to free himself again with his wonderful sword. He then slid back into the water and got away.

The people in the village were so terrified at the strange sight that in all the years that followed, they have never tried to take him again, although fishermen have often seen him since, basking in the shallower parts of the pool. The fish still has the sword girded round him. The legend holds that one day he will give up the sword, but only when the rightful heir of Condover Hall claims it from him; on that day, the sword will be given willingly.

Location: SY5 7AP

Mother Fox's Dream

Throughout the county of Shropshire it is a commonly held belief that if you have the same dream three times, then the dream will come true. However, the converse often happens in practice, hence the saying 'To dream of the dead, good news of the living'; 'Dream of a funeral, hear of a wedding' and 'Dream of a death, hear of a birth'. So, whenever people dream of finding money, it is considered to be bad luck. At least, it's normally considered to be bad luck, but Betty Fox, often referred to as Mother Fox, the wheelwright's wife at Wroxeter, found an abundance of good luck after having dreamt of finding money.

Betty was consumed with the thought of finding treasure at Uriconium; in fact, she went looking for it every day and then dreamt about it at night. One night she actually dreamt that there was a crock of money buried near to an alder bush in the bank on one side of the lane that leads from Wroxeter to Uckington. Her dream was so vivid that she actually woke her husband and told him all about the dream that she'd just had. He didn't believe a word of what she said and told

St Andrew's Church, Wroxeter.

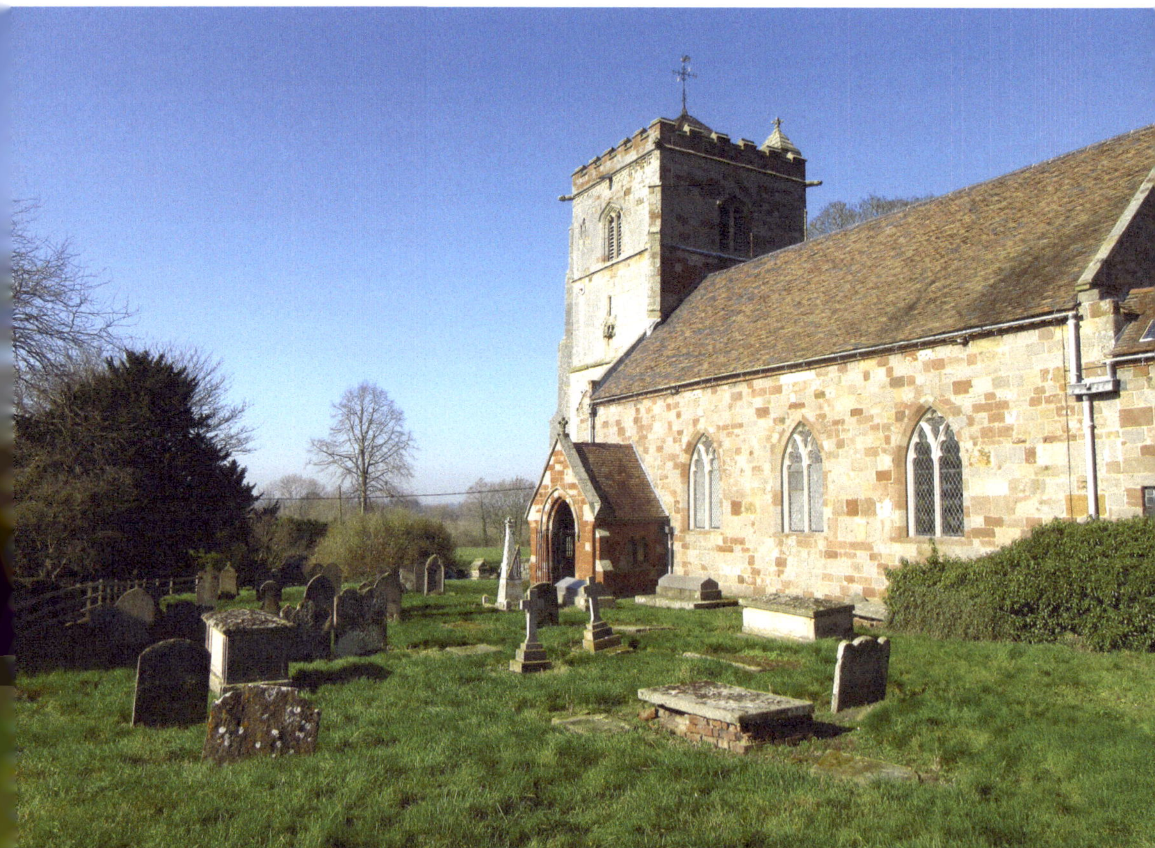

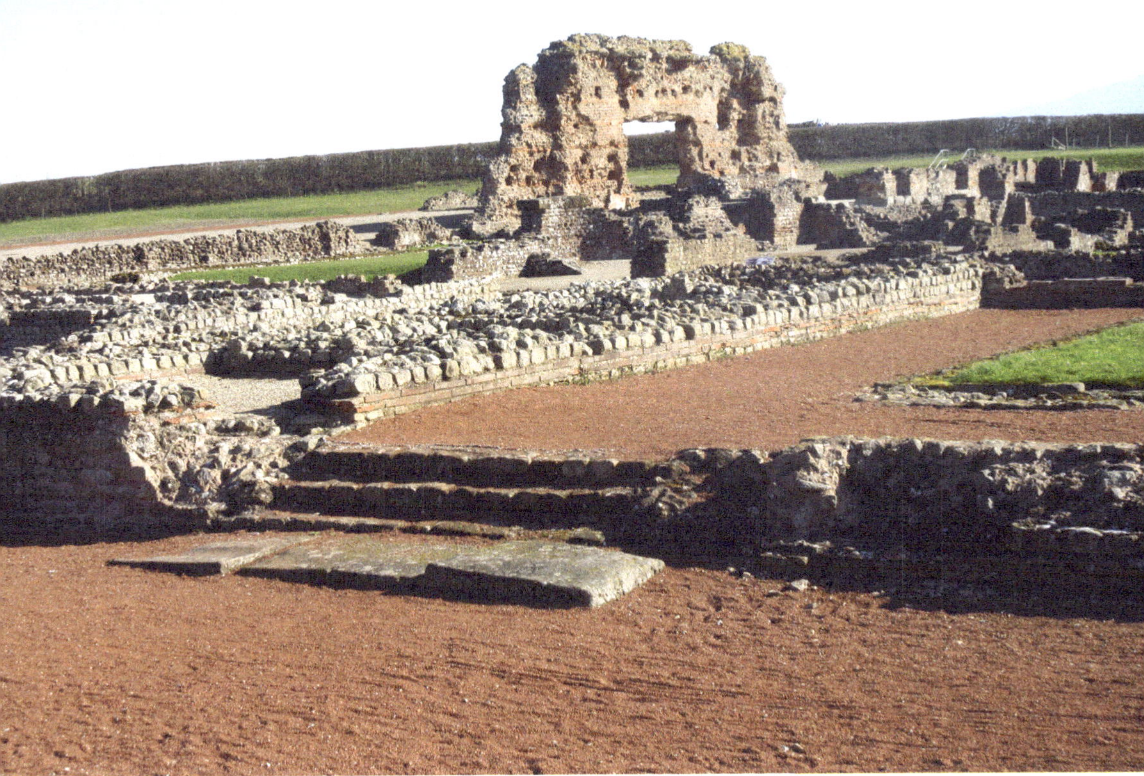

Excavations at Uriconium.

her not to be such a fool and to go back to sleep. Once she'd fallen asleep, she had exactly the same dream as before. It was a waste of time waking her husband again, so she did no more than get up, get herself dressed and set off with a spade in her hand for the place that she'd seen in her dream, even though it was only three o'clock in the morning.

She'd only been digging for a short while under the alder bush when her spade smashed into and broke a Roman earthenware vessel. As it smashed, a great number of silver coins, perhaps as many as 400 in total, came rolling out of the smashed vessel. Mother Fox couldn't believe her luck, and started to gather up the coins in her apron straightaway, taking care not to be seen by anyone who might be in the area at that hour. As soon as she'd collected all of the coins she hurried home to tell her husband the good news: 'Well, fool or no fool, I've found the coins!' Her husband could only stare in disbelief as she emptied her haul onto the kitchen table. Later that day she sold the coins for £30.

Some months later Betty's son was employed on the excavations at Uriconium, but he cannot have been very good at his job. More often than not he was found digging in an area quite different from the place where he had been directed to dig. When challenged as to why he was digging somewhere different from where he'd been asked, his usual reply was that he'd dreamt that there was hidden treasure elsewhere and he was merely following his dream!

Location: SY5 6PH

The Night of Crawls

Not too far from Bromfield Vicarage on the banks of the River Terne and opposite to Oakley Park, there is a magnificent piece of meadowland. Studying the field with a well-trained eye, it is just possible to detect the remains of the moated house that once stood on that site. The field itself is called 'Crawls', and there was at one time a very famous ballad sung telling how the field became known by such a strange name. The words of the ballad have long since been lost and forgotten, but the story of how the field got its name is still told in the village.

The story tells of a young lady who lived in the house many years ago. She was her father's only child and heiress, and he loved her dearly. As the beautiful young girl grew up into a charming young lady she was wooed by a gallant knight who sought her for his bride. She, in turn, loved him dearly and accepted his offer of marriage. Although they kept their tryst a secret, her father did eventually learn of their plans and refused to grant his permission for the wedding to go ahead. He'd learnt that the knight was the younger son of his father and, as such, would not inherit any lands or property when his father died. The young lady's father flatly refused to countenance any relationship between the knight and his daughter. Such intransigence on the part of her father only served to make the young lady more resolute and determined to proceed with the wedding. Summoning all of her courage, she told her father that she was to be married the next morning at Bromfield church. Upon hearing this news, her father was incandescent with rage.

Below left: Church of St Mary the Virgin, Bromfield.

Below right: Bromfield Manor.

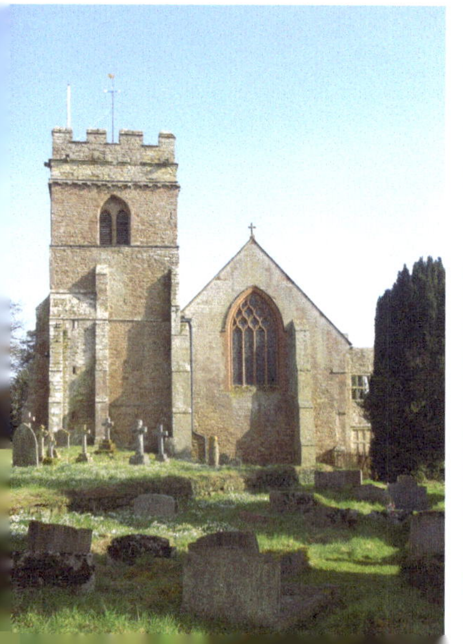

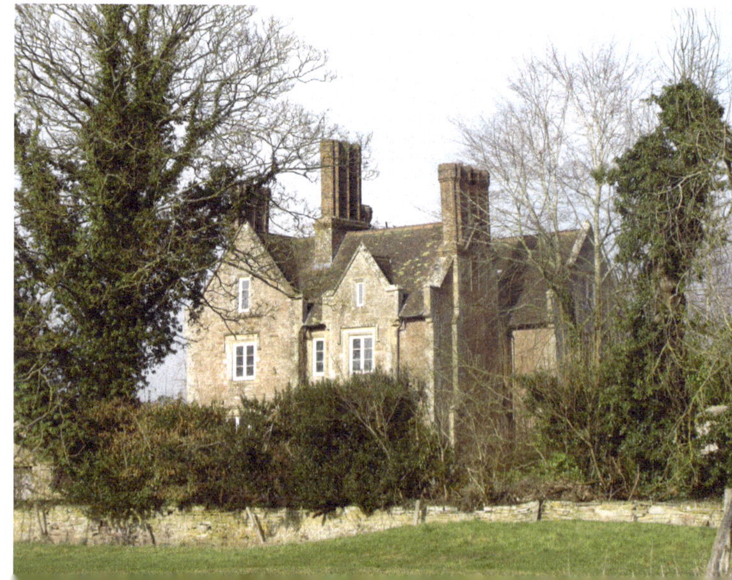

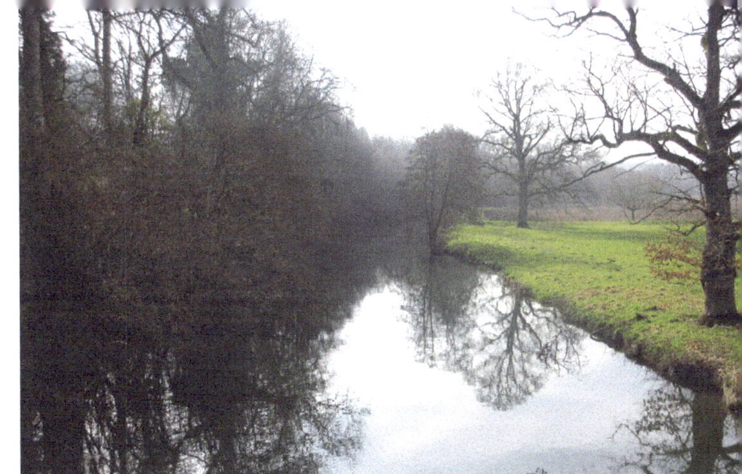

River Terne opposite to Oakley Park.

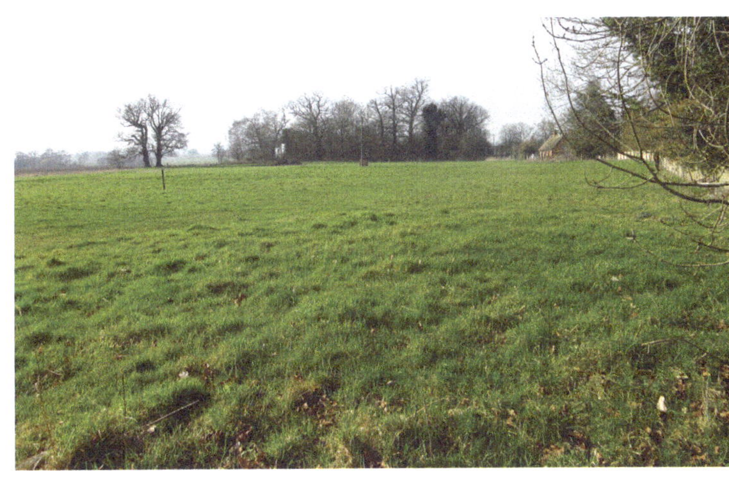

The 'Crawls'.

He admonished her for daring to take such a decision without either his knowledge or approval, telling her that by taking this course of action, she would not inherit any of his vast estates apart from any that she might be able to crawl around before morning light. She gave no reaction to this dictum, but quietly withdrew from her father's presence. She spent some time talking to one of her father's servants who then brought her a pair of leathern breeches that would help to protect her knees during the mission that she was about to embark upon. Duly attired, she set off to crawl around the fields all through the dark, cold winter's night.

As day dawned the mud-covered young lady hobbled into the house where her father was about to start eating his breakfast. Before he had time to question her, she told him that she had taken him at his word and during the night she had crawled around a goodly area of meadowland almost as far as Downton. Upon hearing this news, her father was so delighted and proud of his daughter's strong spirit that all thoughts of her being disinherited were forgotten. She was once again made his heiress and later that very same day married her knight with her father's blessing.

The estates continued to belong to her descendants for many generations, and the land that she had crept around during that long, cold night still bears the name of 'Crawls'.

Location: SY8 2JP

The Last Public Hanging at Shrewsbury Gaol

On the afternoon of Sunday 22 December 1867, nine-year-old Catherine Lewis visited the home of Mrs Ann Davies before attending Sunday chapel. John Lewis and his second wife had five children, of whom Catherine was the eldest. Immediately before leaving Mrs Davies's home, Catherine asked her to pin a brooch belonging to her step-mother onto her shawl.

Directly after the end of the service, Catherine left the chapel on Longden Road at 7.30 p.m. Another member of the congregation on that evening was thirty-year-old John Mapp. He was a farm labourer employed by Mr Whitfield of

The Dana Prison, Shrewsbury.

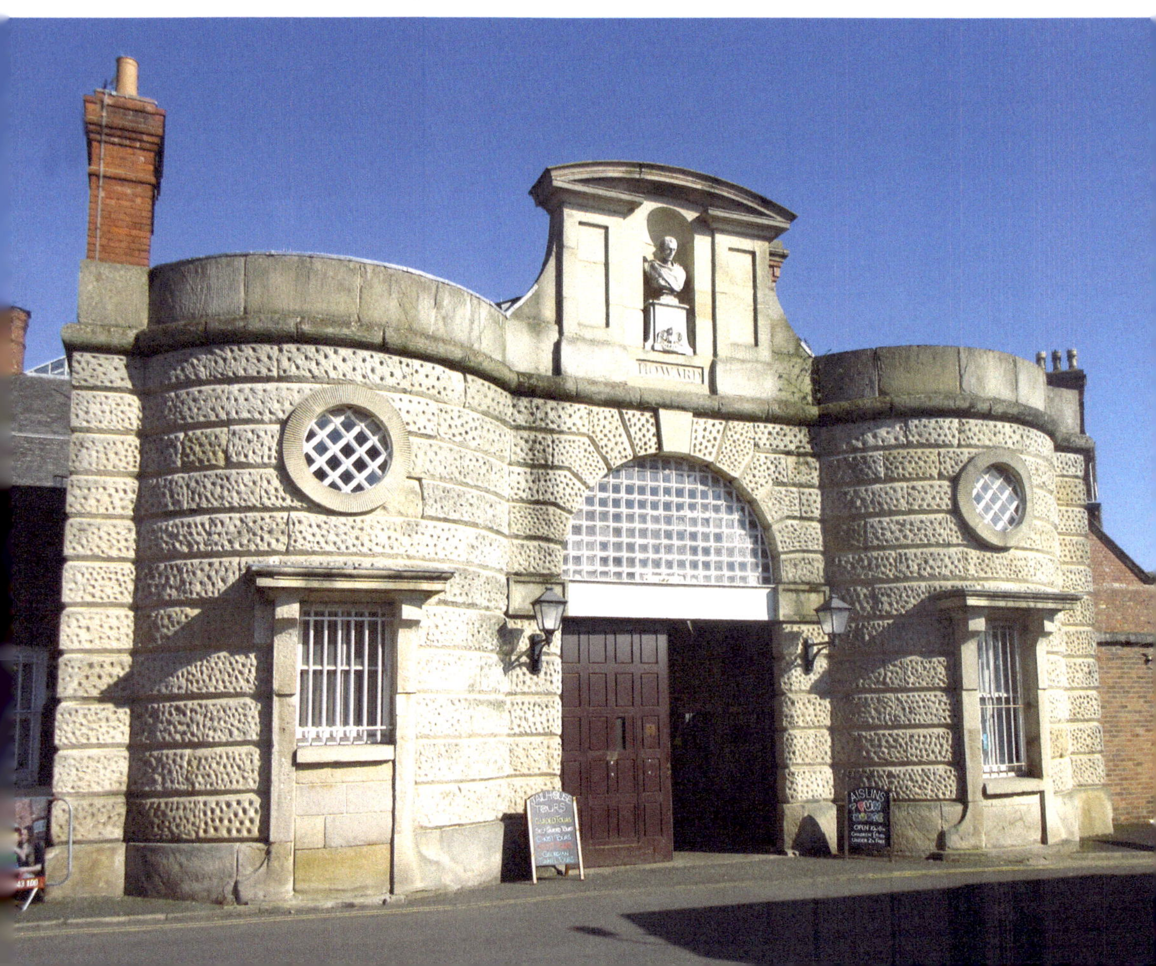

Longden Wood. Among the other chapel goers that evening were Mary Hartshorn and Jane Richards – a domestic servant at the Whitfield farm. Mary left them at Longden Common crossroads while Jane, Catherine and Mapp set off along Long Lane. Jane turned off at Whitfield farm, leaving Catherine and Mapp to carry on down Long Lane.

The following morning John Aston, a waggoner at Whitfield farm, was ploughing a field along Long Lane whilst Mapp was spreading manure. When they stopped for lunch, Aston found a bloodstained black straw hat, which had been stuffed under a bush. Mapp immediately instructed the young waggoner to bury it, but Aston placed the hat near to the entrance of the field. A little while later, Mary Hartshorn, who happened to be passing, thought that she recognised it. She showed the hat to Mrs Lewis who became extremely upset and confirmed that Catherine had not returned home the previous night. When Catherine's father saw the hat he immediately went to look for his daughter. In fact, it was John Lewis himself who found the body, which had been hidden in a derelict hovel. The cruel killer had cut Catherine's throat and then, for some reason, taken the brooch that had been pinned onto her shawl. Catherine's body was taken to the Tankerville Arms where an autopsy was performed.

Suspicion immediately fell on John Mapp as in 1859 he had been transported to Australia for assaulting an old woman. Also, a patch of blood near to the body had been found to be covered in manure. Mapp lived with his parents and when the house was searched a bloodstained knife was found. The brooch that Catherine had been wearing was also found in his coat pocket, so he was arrested immediately.

When Mapp came to trial before Sir Fitzroy Kelly on 23 March 1868, the court was told that Mapp had made sexual advances towards the young girl, but his advances had been refused. He then made a further attempt, which, after sexually abusing her, ended in him suffocating her with her shawl. He then cut her throat and hid her body in a nearby building. The jury had little hesitation in finding him guilty, although he continued to protest his innocence. Mapp did, however, make a full confession the evening before his execution. In making his confession, Mapp related the whole sordid story, claiming that he was sorry for what had happened to Catherine.

Mapp was hanged at 8.00 a.m. on Thursday 9 April 1868. It was estimated that in excess of 5,000 people were present at the execution – the last public hanging to be held at Shrewsbury goal.

Location: SY1 2HR

The Chimneys at Plaish Hall

The Elizabethan Plaish Hall at Cardington is a Grade I listed building. Among many other features of architectural significance, the hall is particularly noted for its fine Tudor chimneys.

Apparently the original house was built of stone, but the new owner, Judge Leighton, the Chief Justice of Wales, was insistent on the hall being rebuilt in brick – the first brick building in Shropshire. When the rebuilding had almost been completed, the pedantic judge insisted that an ornamental chimney builder be employed to add grand ornamental chimneys to the property.

Now Judge Leighton, together with the notorious Judge Jeffries, had both been called 'Hanging Judges', as both had condemned so many people to be hanged. Among that number was a local builder whom the judge had recently condemned to be hanged. Fearing the conviction, the man had journeyed to see the judge in order to plead for clemency. When considering his request, the judge learnt of the man's occupation and suggested that if he would build the finest group of chimneys he had ever built, then his life would be spared and he would be given a lighter sentence. Readily agreeing to the bargain, the builder set about his task with alacrity, and soon a series of beautiful chimneys adorned the house. However, as soon as the work had been completed, the judge reneged on the agreement

Plaish Hall and its famous ornamental chimneys.

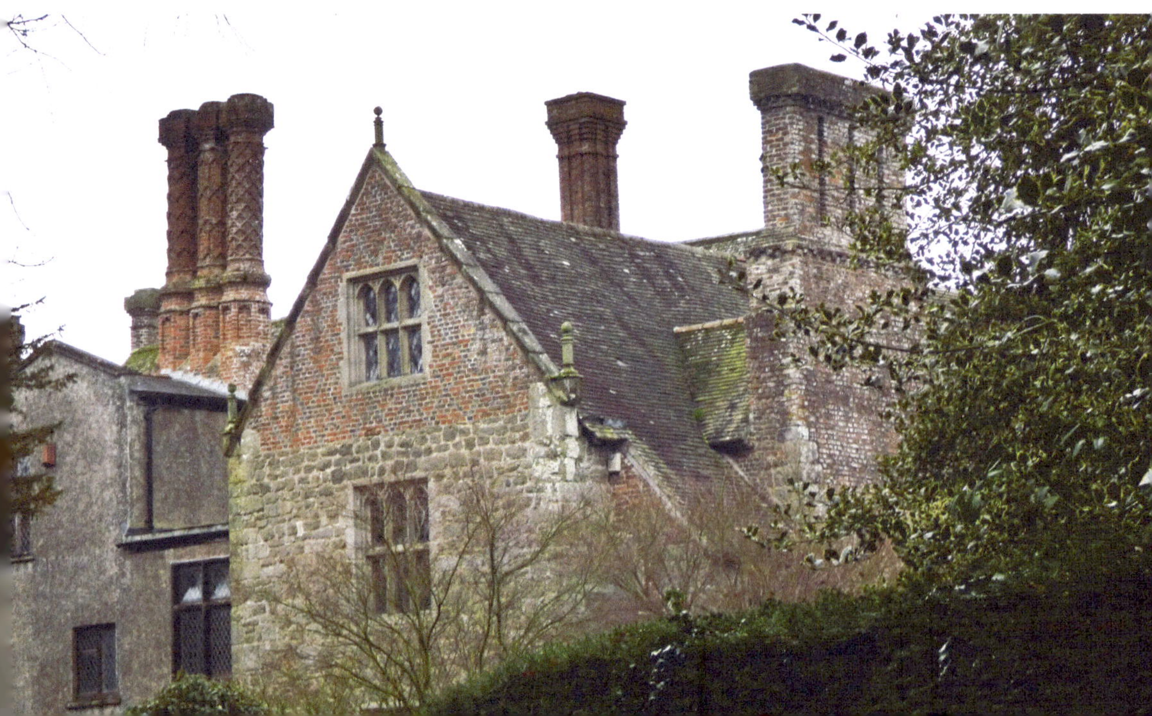

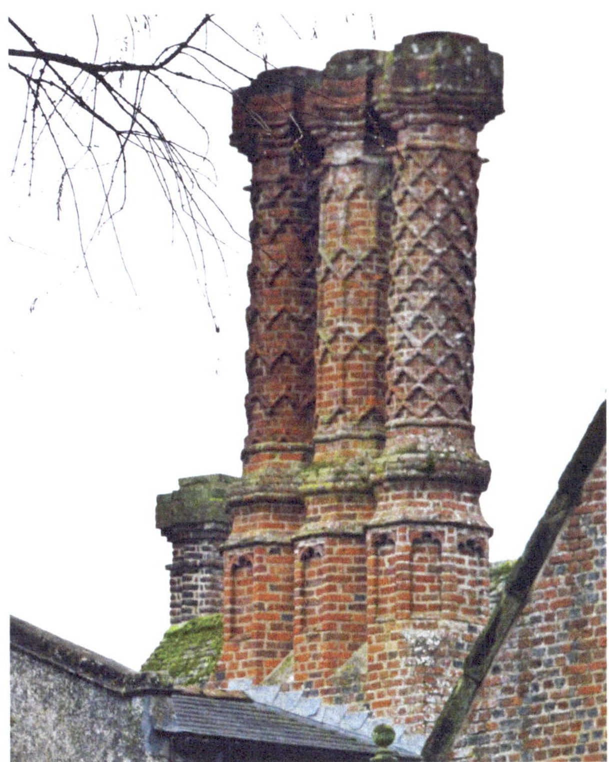

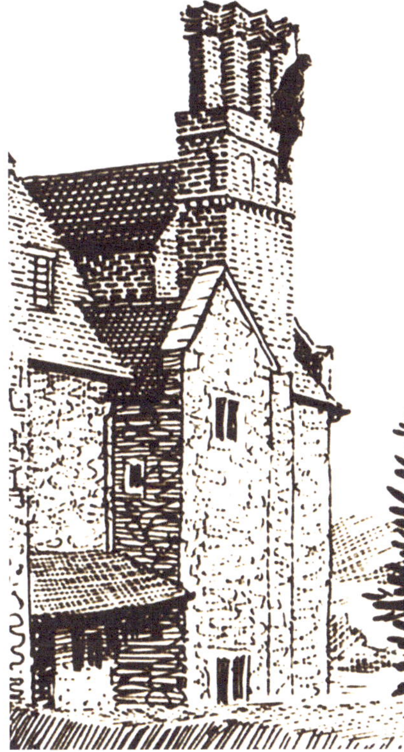

Above left: Ornamental chimneys at Plaish Hall.

Above right: Chimney from where the builder was hanged.

and ordered that the man's eyes should be gouged out, and that he should be hanged from the chimneys that he had just built. To finish the job off so to speak, following the hanging, the judge then had the unfortunate felon entombed in one of the chimney cavities. It is rumoured that on stormy nights, when the wind whistles through the chimneys, the walls of one of the chimney cavities ooze with blood. On other occasions, a Grey Lady, the builder's grief-stricken mother, can be seen walking through the hall accompanied by the spectre of the chimney builder himself. It has also been reported that, sometimes, the rope from which the builder was hanged can be seen dangling from one of the chimneys.

At the time of the outbreak of the First World War; the wife of the owner of the hall died suddenly while, apparently, in perfect health. Her inconsolable husband later rejoined his regiment but was killed shortly afterwards. The property was then left to a nephew, but soon after inheriting the hall, he too met his death in a bad car crash. Ultimately the house was sold by the trustees. Since that time it has changed hands on a number of occasions. At one point a priest was called in to lay the ghost to rest so, hopefully, the evil may have finally departed.

Location: SY6 7HX

Tom Moody – Whipper-In

The small village of Willey is south-west of the town of Broseley. The village itself consists of four farms, with most of the land being owned and leased by the Weld-Forrester family of Willey Hall. During the eighteenth century the village was the site of one of John Wilkinson's ironworks, and the world's first iron boat, a barge, was built there in 1787.

The 'Whipper-In' at Willey Hall in the eighteenth century was Tom Moody. Tom, very much a character in his own right, had a macabre fear of being buried alive.

Tom, a malster's boy, first came to the attention of Squire Forrester when he was putting a bare-backed, crop-eared cob at a gate. What impressed the squire was that he kept him at it until the cob went over. Tom was immediately taken into the Willey stables, riding the Willey horses at a rate that made even the hardest riders stare.

There are many stories about Tom's adventures either riding or driving the squire's buff-coloured chaise. On one occasion he came up to the gate and, touching his horse's flank, jumped straight over. On another occasion he tried the

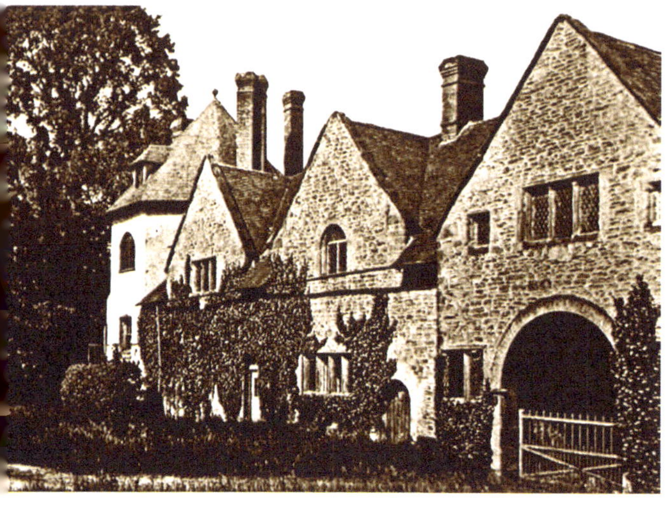

Willey Old Hall.

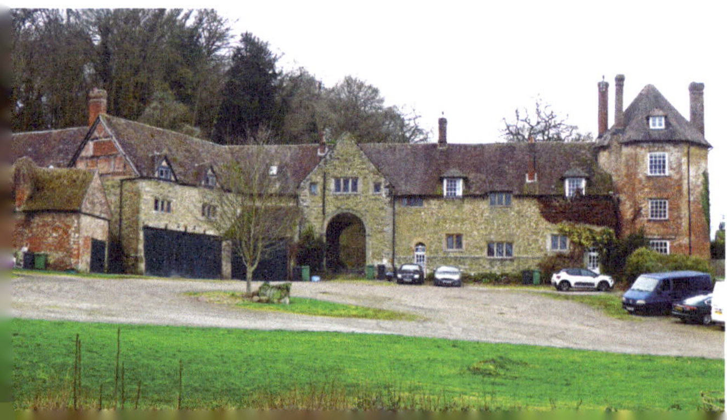

Willey Old Hall today.

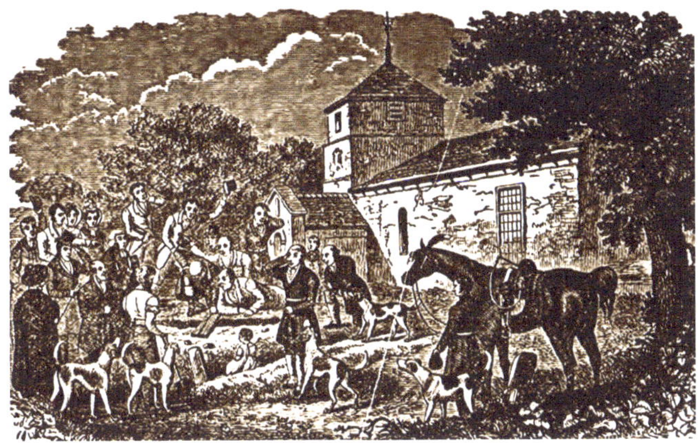

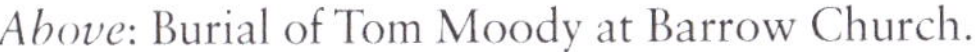

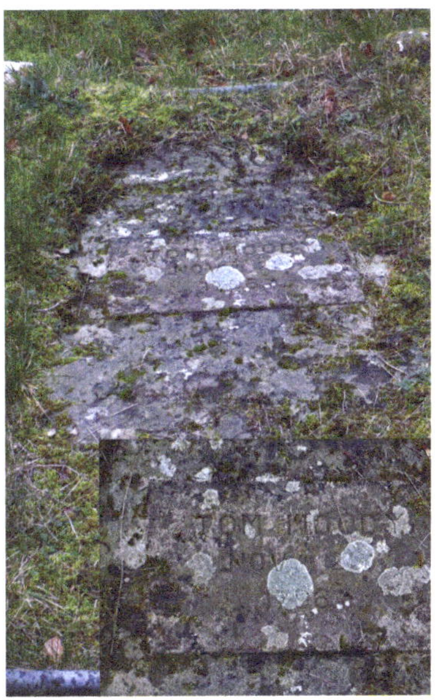

Above: Burial of Tom Moody at Barrow Church.

Right: Tom Moody's grave at Barrow Church.

same trick when driving the buff-coloured chaise, but failed; the horse went clean over, but the gig caught the top rail, and Tom was thrown on his back.

Locals believed that he was like a winged Mercury, making light of both stone wall and high gates. Many believed that he was a regular centaur, for he and his horse seemed as one, but it was in his role as 'whipper-in' that Tom was best remembered. He had a particularly strong bond with his dogs. When he fell into a deep pit his hounds heard his cries for help and at once set off; Tom was soon extricated. As a result of this experience, Tom developed a morbid fear of being buried alive. Sensing that his time was near, Tom asked his master, Lord Forrester, to grant him one last request, and that was to check and see if he was just sleeping before he was laid 6 feet under.

His specific wishes were laid down:

> When I am dead, I wish to be buried at Barrow under the Yew trees, in the churchyard there. And to be carried to the grave by six earth stoppers and my old horse, with my whip, boots, spurs and cap slung on each side of the saddle. And the brush of the last fox when I was up at the death at the side of the forelock, and two couples of old hounds to follow me to the grave as mourners. When I am laid in the grave, let three halloos be given over to me and then, if I don't lift my head, you may fairly conclude that Tom Moody is dead.

Old Tom's premonition was wrong, although his wishes were carried out to the letter. After being called three times he did not stir, so he was duly buried. The slab that covers his grave reads: 'Tom Moody. Buried Nov. 19th 1796'. Tom's spectre can still be seen in the village, his faithful hound at his side.

Location: TF12 5JJ

St Oswald's Well at Oswestry

Although the famous well at Oswestry carries the name of St Oswald's Well, it is thought that the saint himself had very little knowledge, if any, of the well. It is thought that the well was a sacred pagan spring long before the saint's time. However, as early as the fifteenth century, it was recorded that in 'the plain of Maserfeld (Maserfield) the White Church was founded in honour of St. Oswald, and, not too far away there was an unfailing spring, colloquially known as St. Oswald's Well'.

A plaque on St Oswald's Well bears the inscription: 'Legend states King Oswald was killed in battle against King Penda at the Battle of Maserfield. An eagle lifted, flew and then dropped his arm at this site from whence a spring of water has since bubbled.' The stone plaque goes on to state that, 'A scheme of improvements to the well and surroundings was undertaken by Oswestry Town Council and completed in 1985.' The statement concludes, 'Oswestry Town Mayor Councillor J. E. Field.' However, a far more graphic account was recorded by Simeon of Durham in 1882. His account reads:

> the arm, with its consecrated right hand, fell on the bare hard rock. All at once, through God's wonderful power, from the spot where the holy arm touched the ground in its fall, there gushed out a clear unfailing spring. It so happened that Oswin the king, prompted by a message from God, found his way to this spring. He took the arm and hand out of its waters, and as the vision had commanded, he bore away the most holy head with its arms and hands. On this spot, right up until today, miracles are worked through the power of God and the merits of St Oswald. Here sick people receive the gift of health; the mad who come here are freed of their demons; and through drinking the consecrated waters, many kinds of illness are redeemed.

A small stream runs from the well forming a shallow pool a little way below and, following Simeon of Durham's account, prompted a local antiquary in the mid-nineteenth century to write: 'the feeble and the infirm still believe and bathe in the well, and did more so until it was enclosed in the noisy playground. Bottles of its waters are carried to wash the eyes of those who are dim or short-sighted, or the tardy or erring legs of such as are of weak understandings'.

Although the well is now viewed as a local wishing well, there are still those who believe that it has other miraculous powers, primarily associated with the lovelorn. The myth persists that anyone who visits the well at midnight can have their wish granted if, after taking some water from the well in one hand and drinking some of it, then throws the remainder over the well to fall upon a particular stone near to

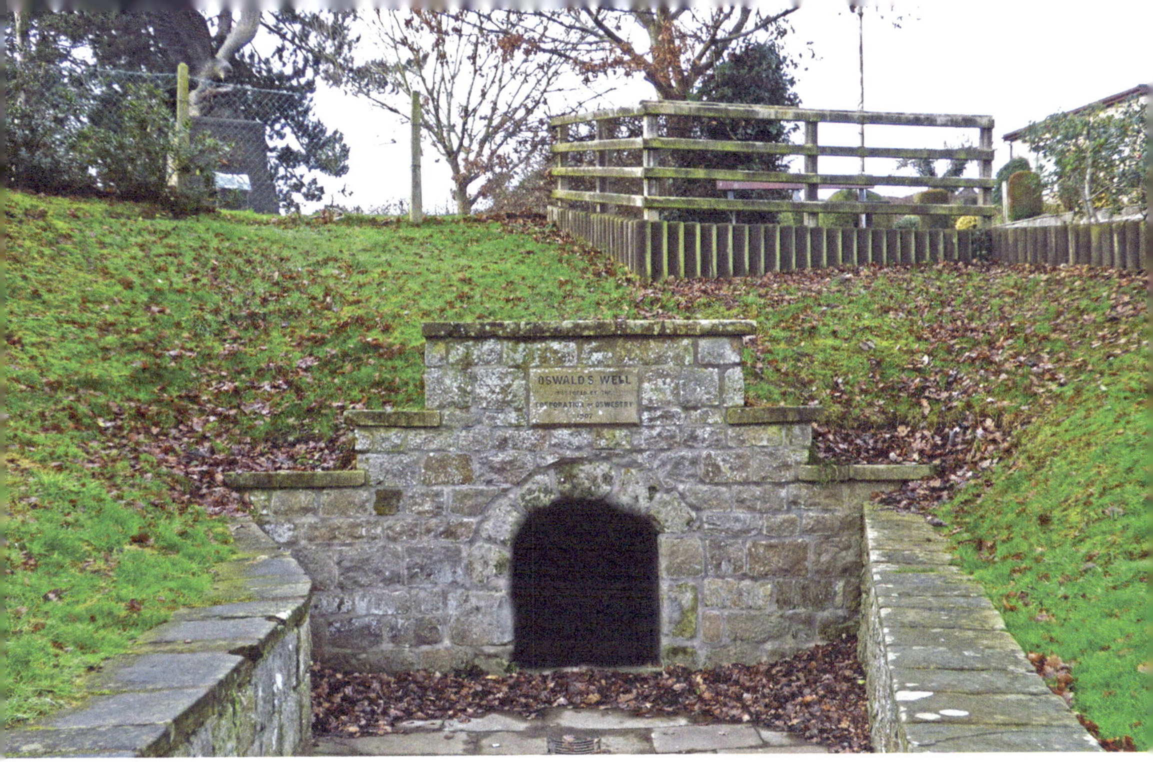

Above: St Oswald's Well at Oswestry.

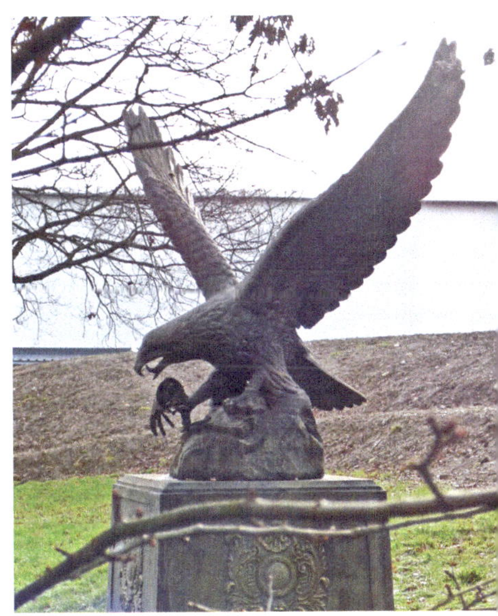

Right: St Oswald's avenging eagle.

the back of the well, without touching any other spot. While performing this ritual, the lover must make a wish as to their preferred outcome.

Other myths persist; for instance, it is still believed by some that wishes can be granted if one bathes one's face in the pool while making a wish. Similarly, if an empty beechnut husk, which bears some resemblance to a human face, is tossed into the pool, a wish will be granted if the husk floats, face upwards, for more than twenty seconds.

Location: SY11 2TP

Major's Leap at Wenlock Edge

Running south-west to north-east across the southern half of the county between Craven Arms and the town of Much Wenlock, Wenlock Edge is a ridge of limestone some 1,083 feet above sea level and over 19 miles (31 km) in length.

Wilderhope Manor was built 7 miles (11 km) south-west of Much Wenlock in 1585 for Francis Smallman. During the Civil War, which lasted from August 1642 until September 1651, the Smallman family was still resident in the manor, the head of the family at that time being Major Thomas Smallman, a staunched Royalist. Smallman, one of Charles I most loyal and ardent supporters, was an officer fighting for the Royalist cause.

When in possession of some particularly important despatches, he was forced to flee from the manor as Cromwell's troops were rapidly approaching, and it was obvious that he was in imminent danger of having to surrender the documents. Travelling alone for both speed and secrecy, Smallman was nevertheless cornered by the Roundhead troops on Wenlock Edge.

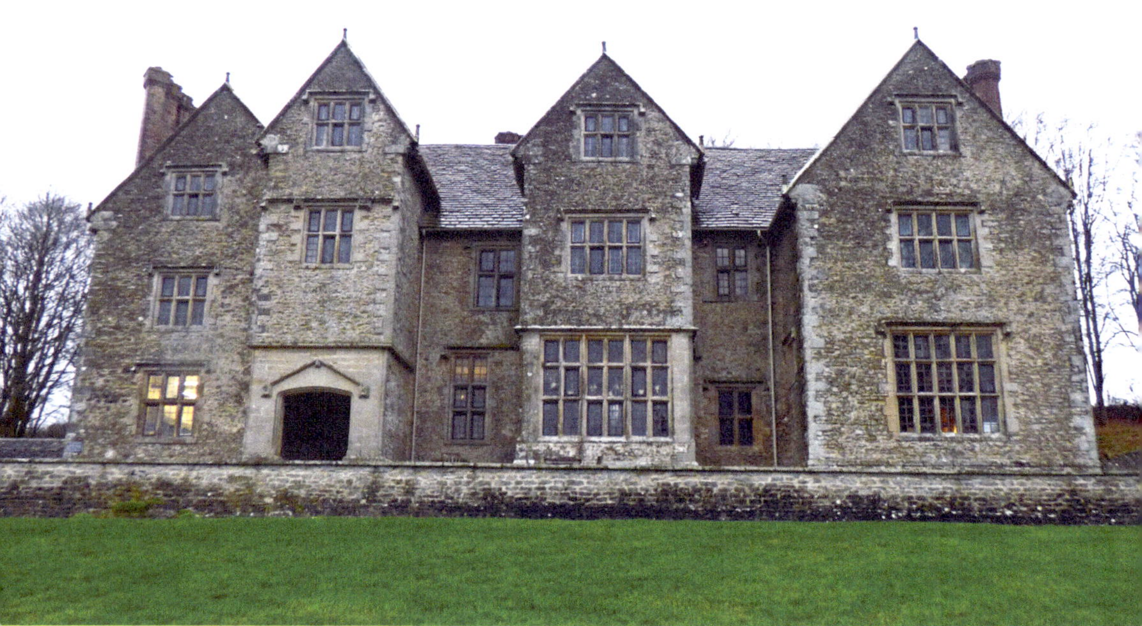

Wilderhope Manor.

Realising the extreme importance of the secret despatches, and having no other means of escape, rather than surrender, he galloped straight to the edge and leapt off, falling through a distance in excess of 200 feet. When Smallman's enemies witnessed his foolhardy act, making his near-impossible leap over Wenlock Edge, they abandoned their pursuit, believing that there would be no way in which he could survive such a leap of complete and utter madness. In fact, Smallman's horse perished in the leap but, miraculously, he survived, breaking his fall on a crab apple tree jutting out from the rock. Although shaken and possibly concussed for a little while, his injuries were nonetheless superficial. After ensuring that the Roundheads were no longer in pursuit and recovering his faculties, Major Smallman made his way on foot to the Royalist stronghold of Shrewsbury, where he delivered his despatches. Then, just a few hours later, as a direct result of his heroic deeds, Royalist forces were able to mount a counter-attack on the Parliamentarians, in which they comprehensively succeeded in utterly vanquishing them.

As the years passed, more and more people were seeing what they believed to be the ghost of Major Smallman, together with that of his horse. Many have reported their ghosts being seen at what has become known as 'Major's Leap', in recognition of his incredible jump, while others have reported the ghosts as having been seen in the manor itself.

The Smallman family continued to own the manor, the Wilderhope farm and the Wilderhope estate until 1734. The manor house was not used as a residence following the sale of the estate.

Location: TF13 6EG

Bridgnorth School

Bridgnorth School has a very long and proud history within the local and wider community of Shropshire.

In 1503, during the reign of Henry VII, Bridgnorth Endowed School was founded and established as a 'common school' by the Corporation of the Borough of Bridgnorth. Initially, the school was supported by the revenues of the Chantries of St Leonard's Church, but later, an annual payment of £8 from the Exchequer was assigned in perpetuity 'to a Schoolmaster keeping a grammar school at Bridgnorth' after the dissolution of the Chantries in 1548.

The school was first housed in a barn that stood on the north side of St Leonard's churchyard outside St Leonard's Church. Previously, the barn had been used as the chapel of St John the Baptist. Towards the end of the sixteenth century the former chapel was becoming known locally as the 'old school-house'.

Unfortunately by 1821 there were only ten pupils still attending the school, and it was then that 24-year-old Dr Thomas Rowley of Middleton Scriven was appointed as headmaster. Before very long under his leadership, the school's reputation increased and numbers rose to around 150. Successive headmasters did not, however, have Dr Rowley's ability or energy and the school's numbers and reputation began to decline.

In 1909 Shropshire County Council took control of the school after a new grammar school had been built at Northgate in 1908.

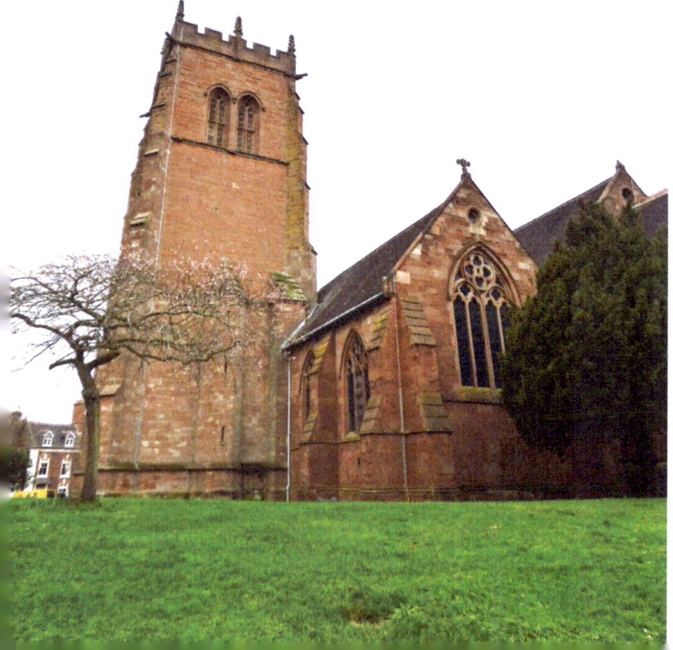

St Leonard's Church, Bridgnorth.

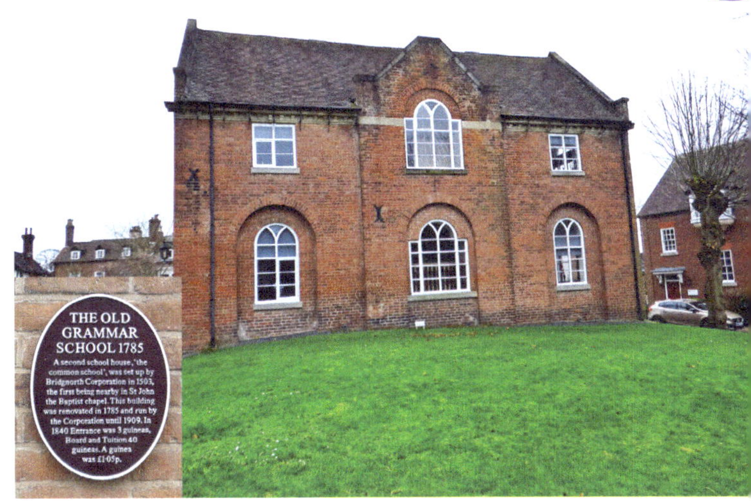

Old Grammar School, Bridgnorth.

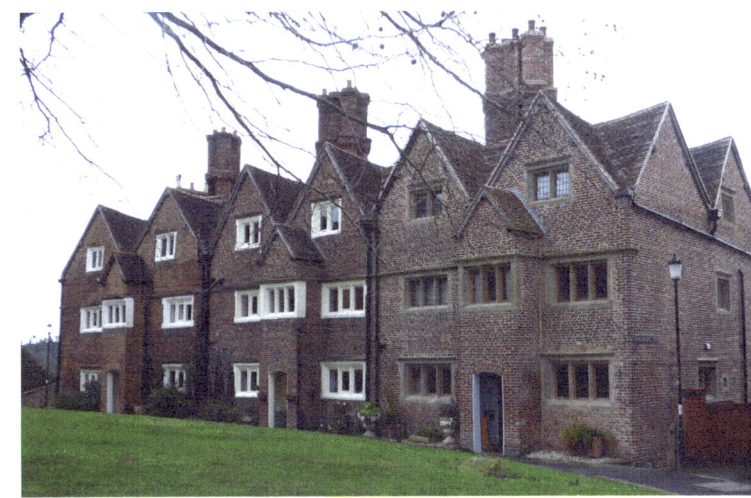

Another former Old Grammar School building, Bridgnorth.

The tale of Bridgnorth School would not, however, be complete without reference being made to the selfless and valiant act of heroism on the part of one of its former scholars. One day during the time when the roof of St Leonard's Church was under repair, two boys from the school entered the site while the workmen were at lunch. Being adventurous boys, they quickly climbed onto the scaffolding, and while busy exploring, a plank upon which they were standing gave way. Both boys lost their balance and fell, but the younger boy managed to hold to a beam. The older boy was also able to save himself by grasping the legs of the other boy. They hung suspended like this for a little while, hoping that the workmen would soon return from their lunch break. However, as time went on the older boy sensed that his friend was beginning to lose his grip. He asked the younger boy if he would be able to hold on a little while longer if he didn't have the added weight on his legs. When the younger boy said that he thought that he would be able to hold on, the elder boy immediately loosed his hold and fell to the floor of the church. It was only a matter of a few minutes before the workmen returned from their break and rescued the young boy, but nothing could be done to save his comrade.

Location: WV16 4ER

John 'Mad Jack' Mytton

John Mytton was born on 30 September 1796 into an aristocratic Shropshire family. His father died when John was just two years old, leaving him to inherit Halston Hall and the estate, together with an estimated annual income in excess of £10,000 – a significant amount in those days.

John was enrolled at the prestigious Westminster School, but was soon expelled for fighting with one of the masters. A little while later at Harrow School he suffered the same fate, on this occasion for leaving a horse in his private tutor's bedroom. He soon acquired the sobriquet 'Mad Jack'.

Having been accepted for Cambridge, Jack prepared by having 2,000 bottles of port sent to his rooms; he left Cambridge before graduating.

Mytton's love of animals was well known. He allowed his favourite horse Baronet to wander anywhere throughout Halston Hall, and very often servants would observe Mytton and 'Baronet' curled up in front of a roaring fire. Mytton also kept around 2,000 dogs, the more favoured ones being fed on steak and champagne. Some dogs even wore livery and others were costumed.

While out hunting in winter, if he became hot during the chase, he would strip off and ride naked.

With his horse pulling a carriage, he once tried to jump over a toll gate to find out whether it was possible. This escapade resulted in some injury to himself and an invoice for a new carriage – the fate of the horse was not recorded.

Taking a fancy to becoming an MP, Mytton 'bribed' his way in by offering £10 to anyone who would vote for him. Having been duly elected, he entered the House of Commons in June 1819, but spent just half an hour in the chamber, deciding that the parliamentary process was too tedious for his tastes! He declined to stand at the next election.

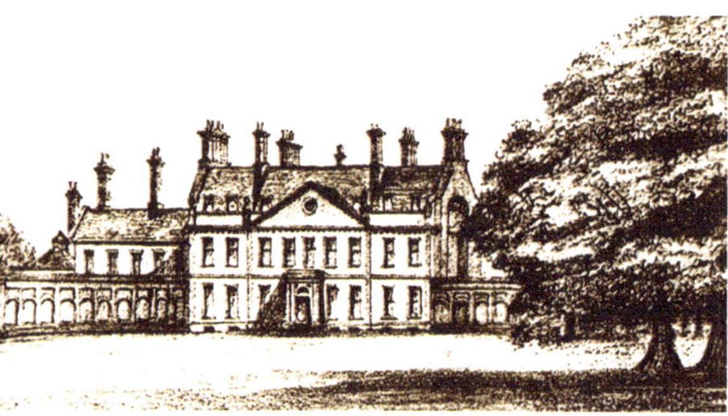

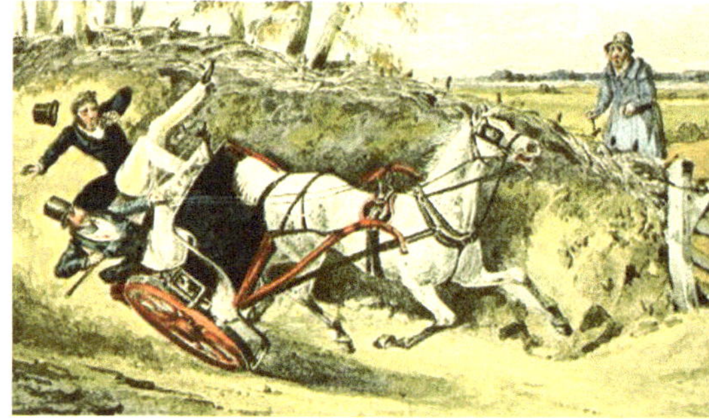

Above left: Sketch of Halston House.

Above right: 'Mad Jack' – wreckless in a gig!

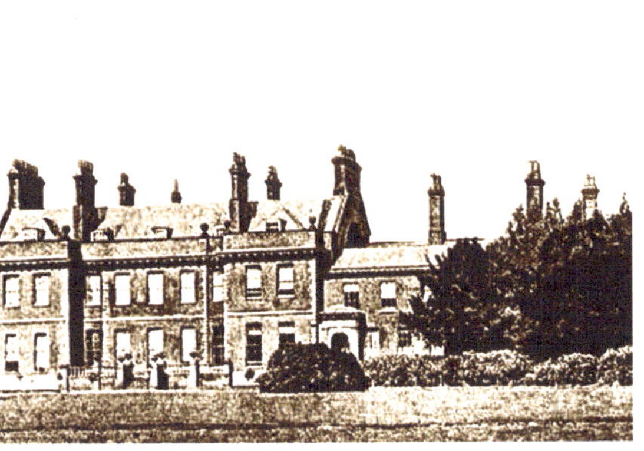

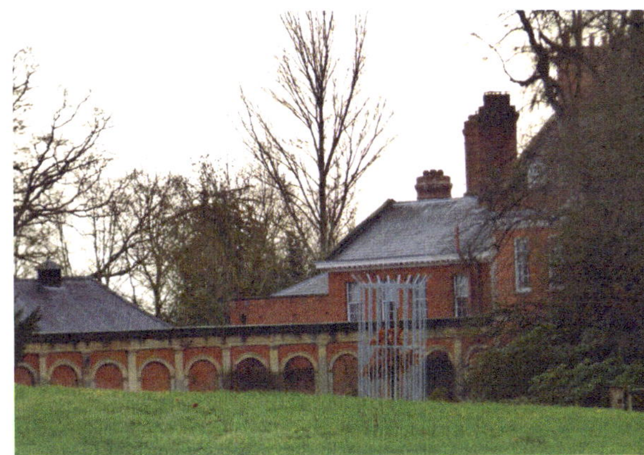

Above left: Early photograph of Halston House.

Above right: Halston House today.

'Mad Jack' was an inveterate gambler. On one occasion in 1826 he accepted and won a wager by riding into the Bedford Hotel in Leamington Spa. He then proceeded to ride up the grand staircase to the balcony, from where he urged his horse to leap over the startled diners below, then through a window and finally out onto the Parade. He was also given to wearing only the best clothes. He is believed to have owned at least 3,000 shirts, 150 pairs of breeches, in excess of 700 pairs of hand-made boots and over 1,000 hats.

There is also little doubt that 'Mad Jack' enjoyed alcohol. He reputedly consumed upwards of eight bottles of port every day, together with a significant quantity of brandy. Some attribute his riding a bear into his drawing room, wearing full hunting costume, to have been fuelled by drink. Apparently, the only damage he suffered was a nip on his leg when he decided to dig his spurs into the bear's side, although one of his servants didn't get off quite so lightly.

Mytton appears to have had a laissez-faire attitude towards money. Visitors to the estate would often find bank notes lying around all over the place, which they were allowed to keep. After fifteen years of uncontrolled spending, 'Mad Jack' had spent the whole of his vast fortune. He fled to France in 1831 with an attractive young woman, hoping to avoid his debtors. While in Calais Mytton suffered an attack of hiccups. He decided that the best cure was the old remedy of 'a fright'. He promptly set his nightshirt on fire! It did the trick and Mytton went to bed naked without batting an eyelid.

When he returned to England in 1833 he was still unable to pay off his debts so he was immediately incarcerated in the King's Bench Prison in Southwark where, in 1834, he died aged thirty-eight. It was estimated that over 3,000 people attended his funeral, mourners included former tenants and servants, serving army officers and many other friends and well-wishers.

Location: SY5 6QH

St Milburga's Well

The eldest daughter of King Merewalh of Magonset and his wife, St Ermenburga, was Milburga. She was the elder sister of St Mildrith and St Mildgytha. The three sisters have often been likened to the three theological virtues of faith (Milburga), hope (Mildgytha) and charity (Mildrith).

Following his conversion to Christianity, King Merewalh founded Wenlock and Leominster priories. He had Milburga installed as the first Abbess of Wenlock. She is reputed to have been a very beautiful, pious woman having remarkable powers that included having the gift of levitation.

There are many different variations of the tale relating to the creation of St Milburga's Well.

One of the more popular variations of the tale suggests that, for some reason, Milburga was forced to live in hiding because she had a number of enemies. Then, one day, her hide was discovered and she was forced to flee. She fled on a white horse, closely pursued by her enemies who were accompanied by a pack of baying hounds. After a long and tiring journey she finally succumbed to her fatigue and fell from her exhausted horse. Her fall was broken when she grazed her head on a protruding rock. She lay unconscious for some while two farm labourers, who had been planting crops in a nearby field, saw her lying, hardly breathing, at the side of her horse. They ran over to render assistance. Very soon they realised that they needed water to bathe her wounds, but there was none to be found. Then, at the saint's bidding, her horse struck the rock with its hoof and, immediately, a spring of pure water burst forth. After having her wounds tended, the saint commanded

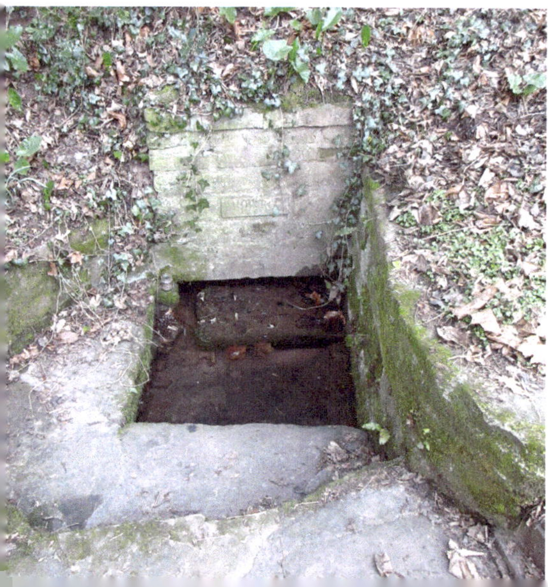

St Milburga's Well.

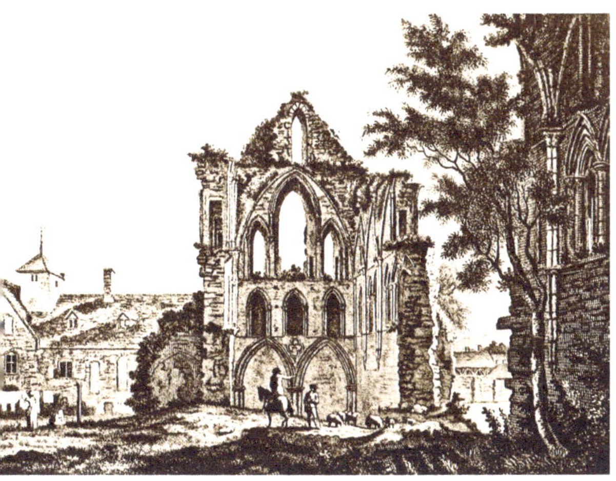

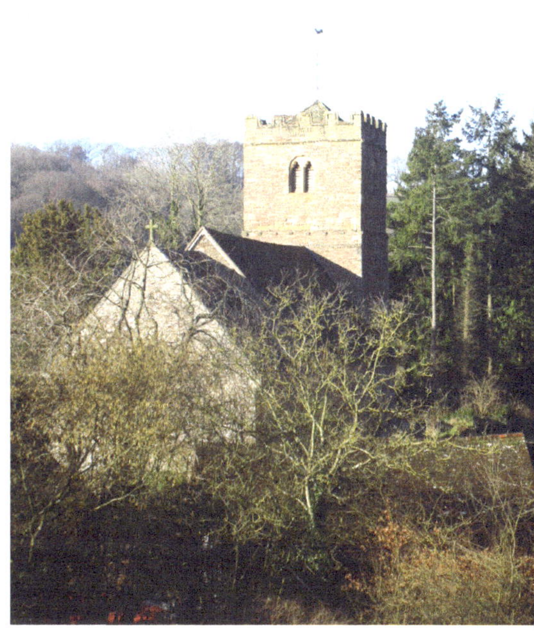

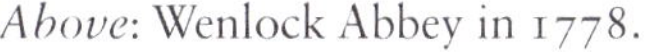

Above: Wenlock Abbey in 1778.

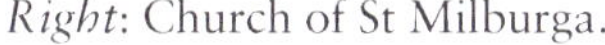

Right: Church of St Milburga.

that from that time onwards, the rock would always be a source of holy water. Before remounting her horse and departing, Milburga caused the barley that the men had just sown to spring up. She then gave instructions to the men: 'When my enemies arrive tell them, truthfully, that they had seen the lady on the white horse pass when they were sowing the barley.' Then, she told the incredulous workers that the barley would be ready for harvesting that same evening. Sure enough, the men found themselves harvesting the barley that night. It was at that time that Milburga's enemies arrived, asking after her whereabouts. They were able to reply, truthfully, that she had passed when they were sowing the barley, causing consternation and bewilderment to her pursuers. The saint's enemies finally accepted the futility of their pursuit when they discovered that the barley had been sown in the morning, ripened at lunchtime and was ready for harvesting in the evening. They accepted that they couldn't fight against the will of God.

Subsequent to this event, the well was bestowed with miraculous powers whereby the sick and ailing could be cured by taking of the waters issuing from the well.

A variation on the tale suggests that St Milburga was admired from afar by a local lord who wanted her to become his wife. When she heard of this, and subsequently refused his advances, he pursued her with a number of his armed staff. Milburga fled, crossing the River Corve, which, as soon as she was on the far side, rose up and barred the way for her pursuers.

Location: SY8 2EJ

The Ghost of Ludlow Castle

Love and deceit are two of the major ingredients that figure in the tale of the Ghost of Ludlow Castle – Marion de la Bruyere.

Records dating from 1138 make reference to Ludlow Castle, but the architecture of the group of buildings including the curtain wall of the inner bailey, together with the flanking towers and parts of the gatehouse keep, suggest that the building of the castle dates from late in the eleventh century or earlier. The castle was strategically located by the rivers Teme and Corve and had steep slopes to both the north and west. The de Lacy family retained the lordship of the manor of Stanton until the late thirteenth century, a role that they had held since 1066.

In 1139 Lady Sybil de Lacy held Ludlow Castle against King Stephen. Wishing to turn Ludlow Castle to his cause, Stephen arranged for Sybil to marry one of

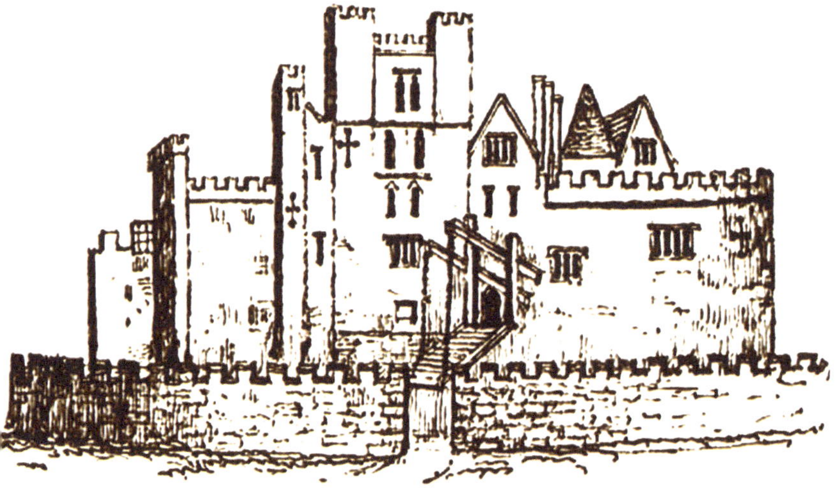

Early sketch of Ludlow Castle.

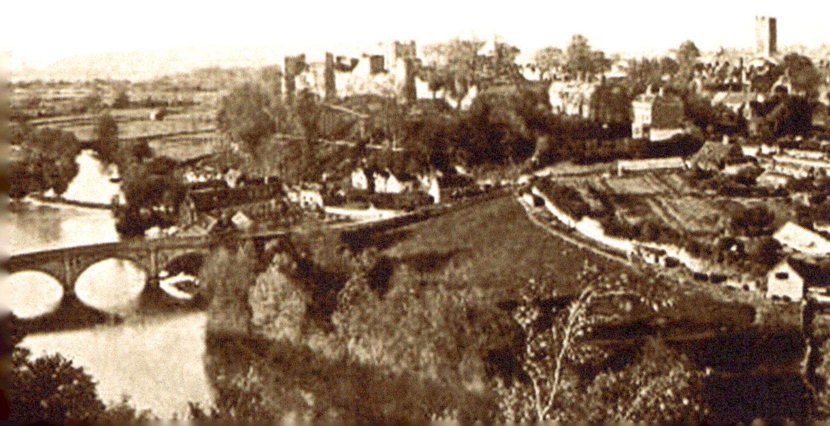

General view of Ludlow, *c.* 1899.

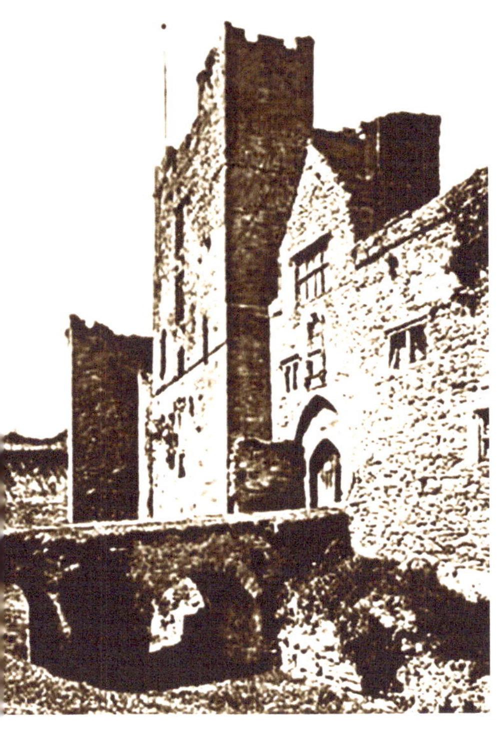

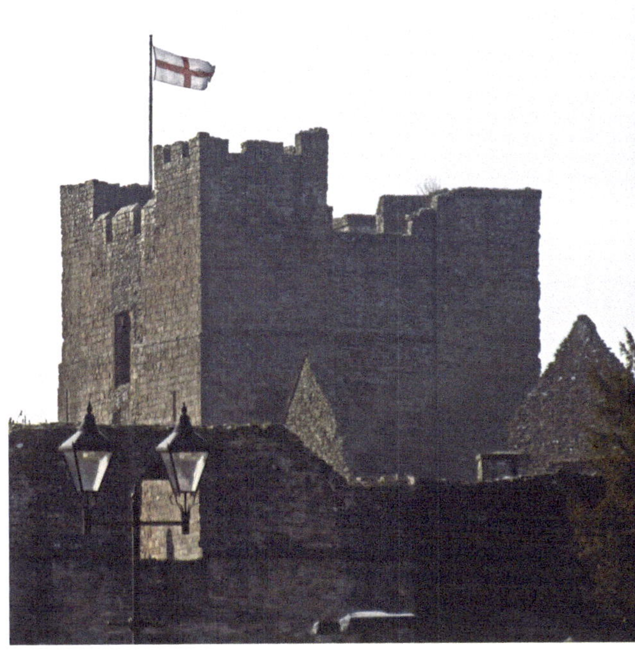

Above left: Early photograph of the keep at Ludlow Castle.

Above right: Ludlow Castle is at the heart of Ludlow life today.

his trusted followers, Josce de Dinan, but in all of the political manoeuvrings that subsequently occurred, Josce de Dinan fortified Ludlow against the king.

It's at this point that Marion de la Bruyere enters the narrative. She was a member of Lady Sybil de Lacy's entourage and lived at Ludlow Castle, but she had fallen in love with Arnold de Lys, one of the king's supporters and an enemy of the castle's lord. Marion had agreed to meet de Lys as the darkness of night was beginning to enfold the castle. From the tower where she was resting, she lowered a rope so that he would be able to climb up and meet her. Unfortunately, the knight had ideas other than love on his mind. For, no sooner had he swarmed up the rope than he enabled over 100 of his men to enter the castle and within a very short time the whole of the castle was crawling with enemy troops and the town of Ludlow was, effectively, in the hands of its enemies. As soon as she realised exactly what was happening and the fact that she had been betrayed by her lover, Marion snatched his sword and without any hesitation cut his throat and killed him. Shortly afterwards, when she had taken time to reflect upon what she had done, she was overcome with grief, guilt and shame, and in a frenzy of remorse for bringing downfall to the castle, she killed herself by throwing herself from the Pendover Tower. She was found dead, impaled upon the rocky outcrop below.

It has been recorded that visitors to the castle in the early evening have testified to having seen Marion's ghost near to the tower. There is also a considerable body of evidence that would suggest that on the anniversary of her suicide, agonised screaming can also be heard near to the place of her fall.

Location: SY8 1AY

Some Traditions in and around Pulverbatch

There were many different celebrations held at various times of the year in Shropshire, including celebrating the 'bark harvest' or the end of the woodcutting and bark-stripping season. One way or another, local people took every opportunity to celebrate as often as they could find a reason to. For instance, whenever people from the neighbourhood in and around Baschurch went to the market at Shrewsbury, they formed themselves into small travelling parties because of the great distance it was to the market itself. Always well prepared for the long journey, they took plenty of food along with them. On the way back, when the time came to rest they settled in a farmer's field to eat and drink, but before embarking on the final stage of the journey, there was always dancing in the field.

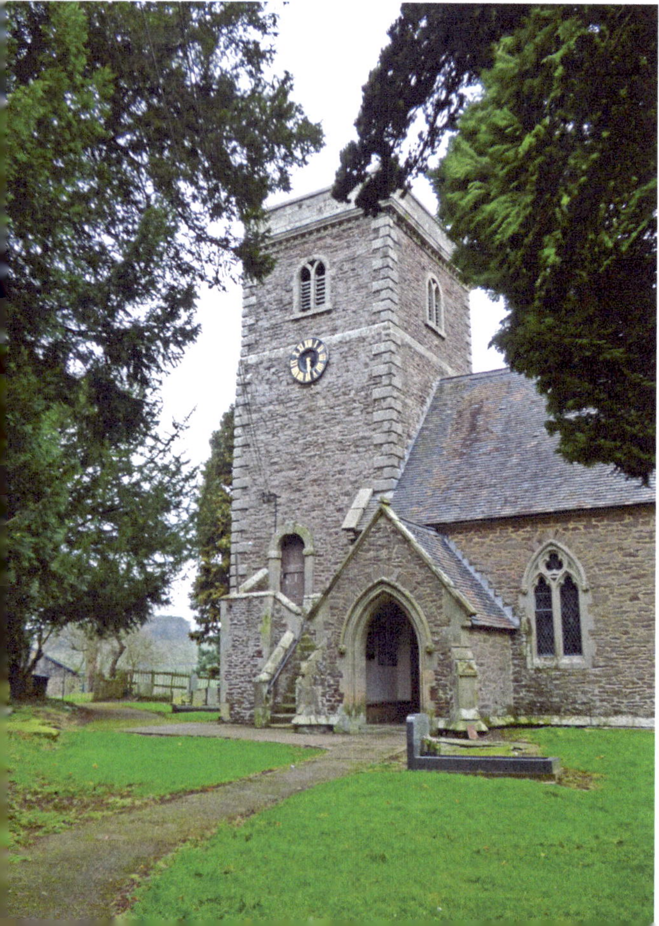

Church of St Edith, Pulverbatch.

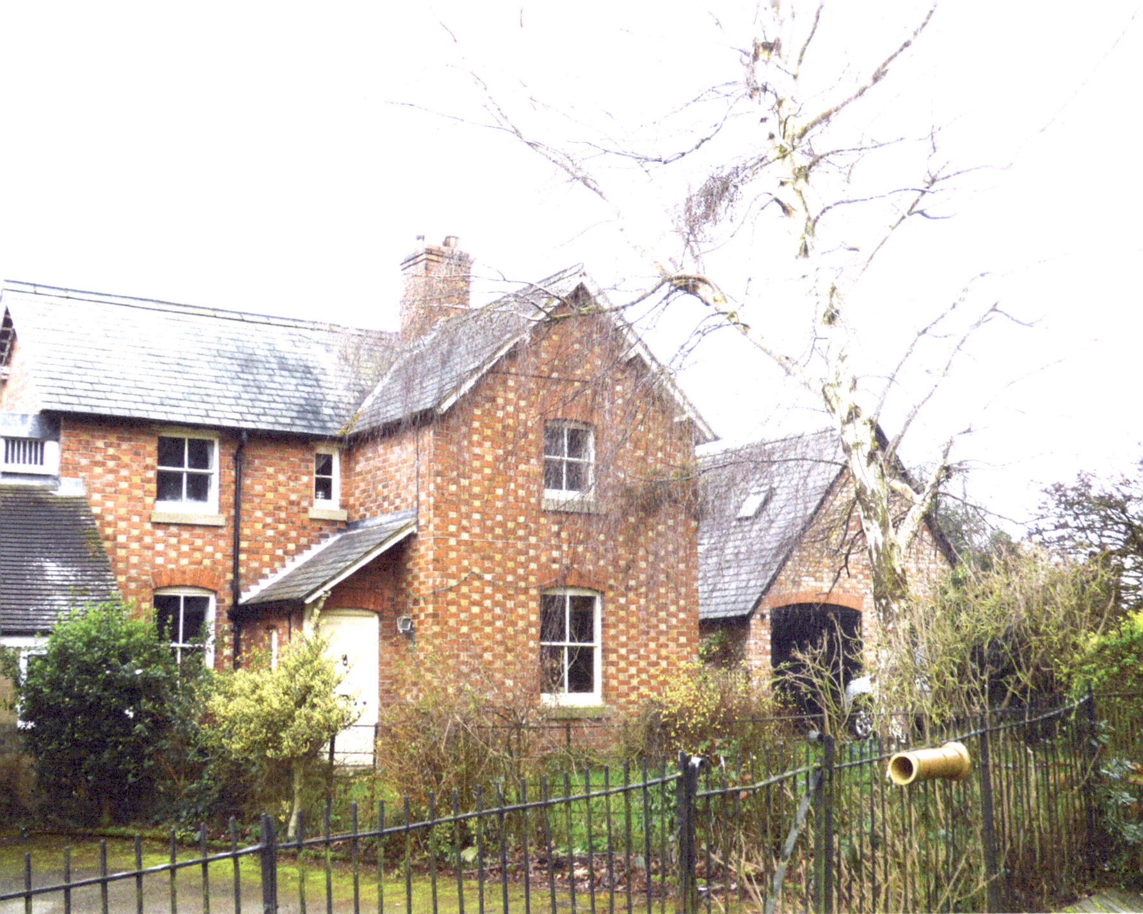

The Old School House, Pulverbatch.

The village blacksmith was an important person in the neighbourhood, not least to the farmers in the area, so once every year all of the local farmers carried all of the coal that the blacksmith would need to keep his furnace going throughout the coming year.

There was little rest for the women of the village, with much of their time taken up by spinning all of the wool that her family might require during the year. Because of the sheer amount of work that this process involved, it was not unusual to fall behind in the task, and it was on these occasions that help would be sought from friends and neighbours. On the agreed day, spinning wheels would be brought along and the rest of the afternoon would be spent spinning thread.

Another custom that was, for many years, practiced at Pulverbatch was the somewhat dubious tradition of 'Caking'. This practice fell somewhere between being a social gathering and an illicit gaming party, with the specific aim of making some money during a particularly barren time of the year. After harvest time, but before Christmastide, women who were proposing to hold a 'caking' made a quantity of small cakes from gleanings gathered from the fields. Neighbours and other farm workers were then invited to come along and spend the evening playing cards for the cakes. Cakes were sold at a penny each and 'them as won got a cake, an' them as lost bought another.' At the end of the evening the hostess

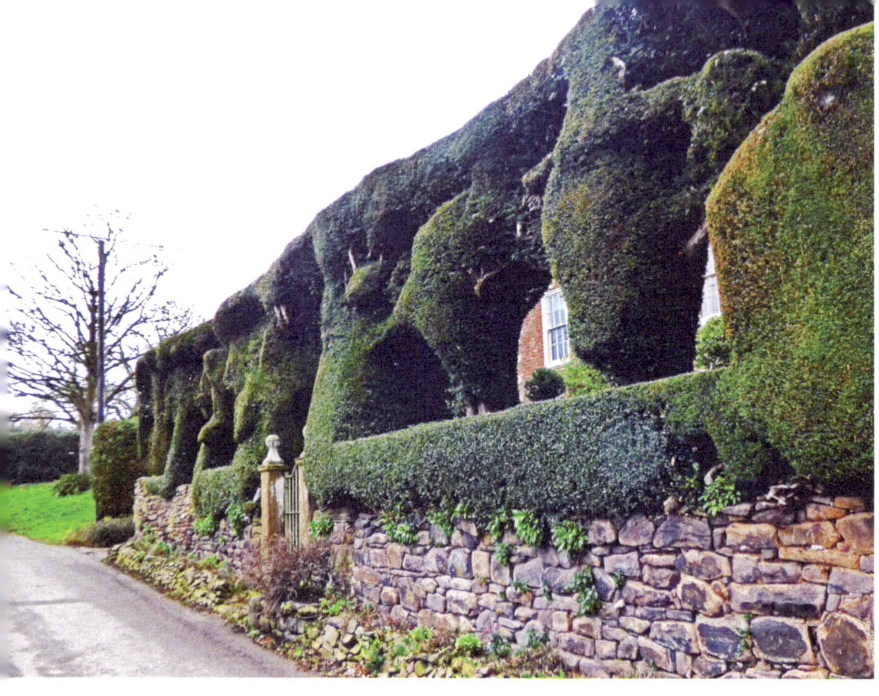

Topiary in Pulverbatch.

bought back the cakes from the winners at the rate of three cakes for two pence and then resold them to the losers at the original price. It was not unusual for the hostess to gain upwards of ten shillings on a successful evening. The practice, which was generally frowned upon, ceased to be a feature of village life towards the end of the nineteenth century.

Another tale often told about Pulverbatch concerns old Betty Chidley who lived in a cottage near to the farm that the Ambler family owned at Wilderley. Betty could often be found begging at the farmhouse and more often than not, she was given some sustenance. On one occasion, Betty came to the farmhouse and noticed that the farmer's wife was mixing some feed, or 'supping', for the newborn calves. Totally absorbed in watching the process of mixing milk and meal being gently stirred together over the fire, Betty thought that she would like to try it and asked to be given some. The farmer's wife said that it was being prepared for the animals and she intended to give it all to them. By way of reply, Betty said 'the calves' wenna eat the suppin' now'. Sure enough, when the milk maid carried the 'suppin' to the calves, they wouldn't drink it even though several attempts were made.

The farmer's wife then remembered Betty's words, so the milk maid was asked to go and fetch her back so that she could bless the calves. At first she was sceptical, 'me bless your calves, what have I to do with your calves?' She finally agreed to Mrs Ambler's pleas and said, 'my God bless the calves,' but the calves still refused to eat the 'suppin'. It was only when Mrs Ambler asked her to just say 'God bless the calves' that the animals started to eat. The Ambler family remembered the event and never again refused to give 'suppin' to old Betty.

Location: SY5 8DF

The Puritan of Moreton Corbet Castle

The story of Moreton Corbet Castle dates back to 1086, when Anglo-Saxon thegns lived at Moreton Toret. Following marriage, the Corbets assumed ownership and also gave their name to the village. Through astute stewardship and deft political acumen, by the start of the sixteenth century the Corbet family was counted as being one of the wealthiest and most powerful families in Shropshire.

Sir Andrew Corbet began to transform the mediaeval castle into a manor house by making considerable modifications to the property. Then when Sir Robert Corbet inherited, he completed the refurbishment. He then started to build a new Elizabethan manor – heavily influenced by classical Italian architecture – but before his plans could be brought to fruition, he died of the plague. The task of completing the building then fell to his two brothers and successors, Richard and Vincent Corbet, who continued with the building of the new manor.

Being a Royalist at the time of the Civil War, Sir Vincent Corbet had allowed his house to become an integral part of the Royalist defences at Shrewsbury, and it is during that time that the tale of Moreton Corbet Castle then takes a different turn. For, during those turbulent times, in addition to political turmoil, religious conflict and dissention were also woven into the mix, causing many prominent Puritans

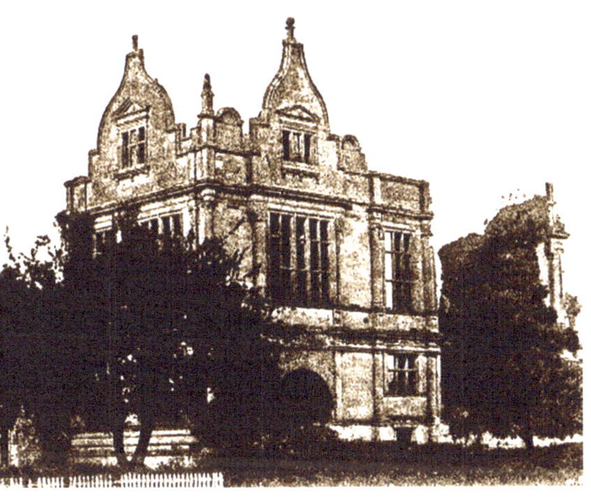

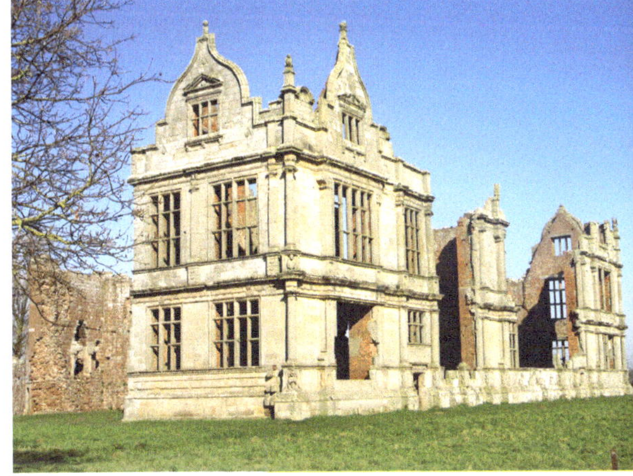

Above left: Moreton Corbet Castle.

Above right: Ruins of Moreton Corbet Castle.

to be subjected to intense persecution. Sir Vincent, although not being a Puritan himself, was conscious of the trials being faced by his friend and neighbour Paul Holmyard, who was a Puritan. In a selfless act of Christian charity, Sir Vincent gave sanctuary to his neighbour. The outcome, it transpired, was not quite as Sir Vincent had envisaged. It appears that during the time of his sanctuary, Holmyard's puritanical views became more fanatical, prompting Sir Vincent to rescind his offer of sanctuary. Holmyard was forced to take refuge in a local wood, living on berries, herbs and whatever could be scavenged from the land. Having survived in this manner for some time he eventually decided to venture as far as Morton Corbet where, quite by chance, he encountered Sir Vincent. His general disposition and frame of mind perhaps prompted his outburst when he uttered the following curse:

> Woe unto thee, hard hearted man, the lord has hardened thy heart as he hardened the heart of the Pharaoh, to thine own destruction.
>
> Rejoice not in thy riches, not in monuments of thy pride, for neither thou, nor thy children, nor thy children's children shall inhabit these halls.
>
> They shall be given up to desolation; snakes, vipers and unclean beasts shall make it their refuge, and thy home shall be full of doleful creatures.

It would appear that Holmyard's curse was fulfilled, in that the curse put so much fear into them that neither Sir Vincent nor his son, Andrew, would ever live in the house again. After years of neglect the once grand house eventually became a ruin.

Local people allege that on dark, moonlit nights the forlorn figure of Paul Holmyard can still be seen wandering around the grounds, ensuring that no building work goes on.

Location: SY4 4DW

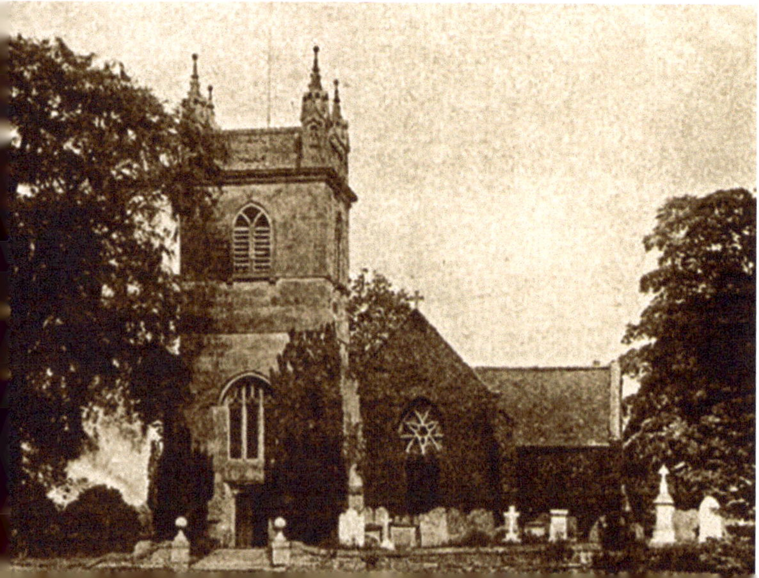

An early photograph of Moreton Corbet Church.

The Bailiffs' Feast at Ludlow

The folk of Shropshire are renowned for their enjoyment of feasts and festivities. Every year on 28 October there was a sumptuous banquet held at Ludlow, known as the Bailiffs' Feast. Also, as tradition dictated, there was a buck hunt on the following day, when a stag was set free in the Old Field, a scene always witnessed by large crowds. Later that evening the bailiff hosted a grand ball and this signalled the start of the Ludlow Assemblies, which were then held every fortnight throughout the winter period. This tradition continued until the Municipal Reform Act of 1835 abolished bailiffs, and, as a consequence, there was no longer a reason to hold the feast.

The Municipal Reform Act also brought to an end the office of bailiff of Much Wenlock. At this town, when there was still a bailiff, it was customary for the retiring bailiff and his newly elected successor to choose two new burgesses. When the appointments had been made, the newly appointed burgesses attended the Bailiff's Feast. Part way through the evening, the top of the ceremonial mace was unscrewed, and a cup that held about one pint was taken out. This was then filled with port wine, and the two new burgesses were required to stand up in turn, propose the toast 'Prosperation to the Corporation', and then empty the cup. The toast is still sometimes made at public dinners at Wenlock.

The time-honoured custom of winding up the list of toasts with the famous Shropshire toast, 'A Health to All Friends Round the Wrekin', was made at the luncheon given by the Mayor of Shrewsbury at the opening of the Free Library on 9 April 1885.

In the land 'between Severn and Clee' there was the old custom of 'dancing Tetheroy.' Whenever a person in a party of drinkers was thought to have passed the bounds of sobriety he would be given the opportunity of 'dancing Tetheroy'. Having accepted the challenge, a lighted candle would be placed on the floor or on a table, and the accused person was required to caper around it without touching it or losing his balance. If he was successful in this feat, he was adjudged to be sane and sober. The wilder the antics he played, and the nearer he approached to the flame, the better the test, proving:

A man is neither drunk nor mad
If he can dance Tetheroy, Tetheroy!'

Location: Throughout Shropshire

Strange Happenings at the Tontine Hotel

The small town of Ironbridge, which lies at the heart of the Ironbridge Gorge on the River Severn, takes its name from The Iron Bridge which spans the river at that point. The 100-foot bridge, the first of its kind in the world, was constructed in 1781. It was in this area, at Coalbrookdale, that Abraham Darby perfected the technique of smelting iron with coke, which considerably reduced the cost of producing iron. Construction of the bridge, designed by Thomas Farnolls Pritchard, started in 1779 and it was opened on New Year's Day 1781.

The bridge attracted much interest, and when the owners saw the commercial possibilities they built the Tontine Hotel to cater for the ever-increasing numbers of visitors.

Tontine Hotel, Ironbridge.

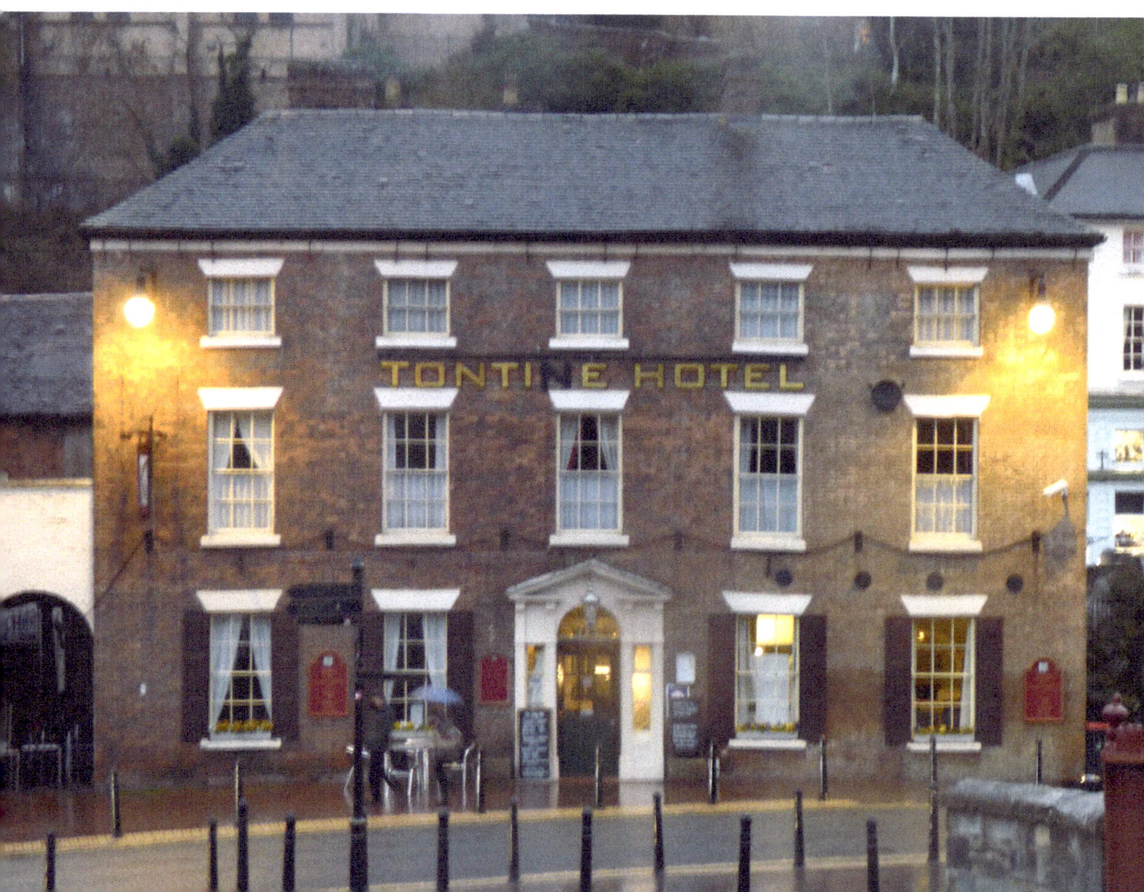

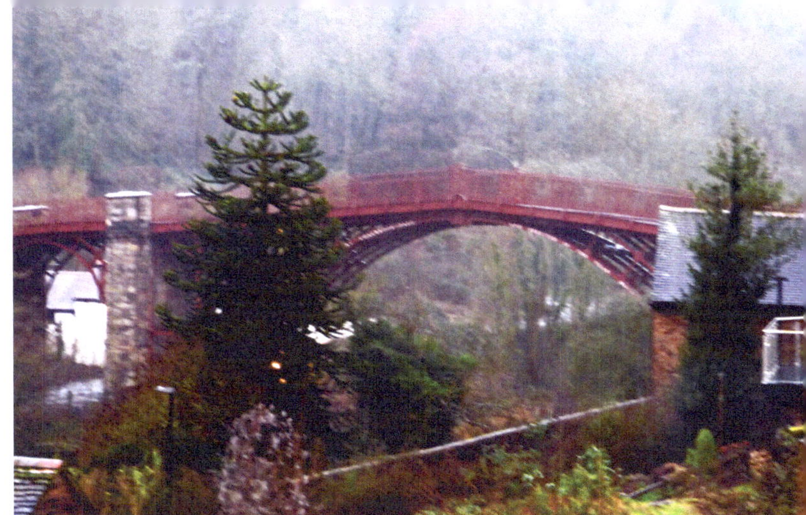

The Iron Bridge, the world's first cast-iron bridge, opened in 1781.

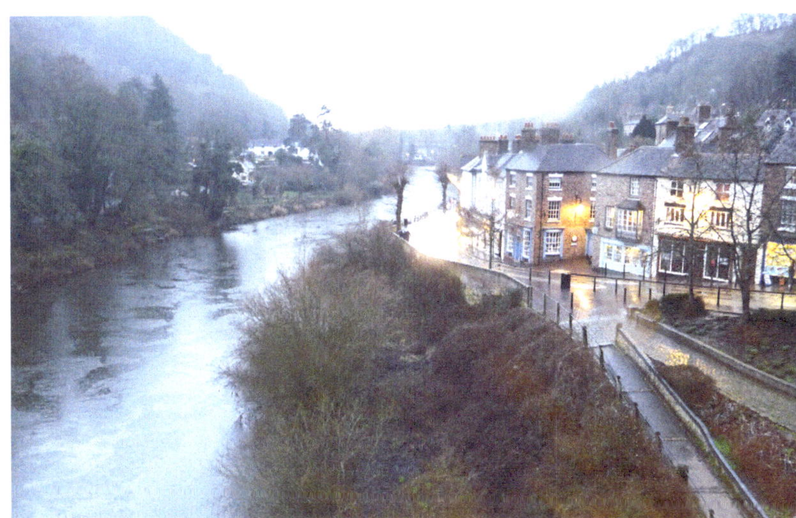

The River Severn at Ironbridge.

During the 1950s, the hotel attracted some unwanted publicity, as it was place where police arrested Frank 'Fred' Griffin. Griffin, who was living at the Tontine Hotel, murdered his landlady at a house in Ketley. He then went back to room five at the hotel, and it was there that the police eventually arrested him. Griffin was tried and then hanged in Shrewsbury. Since that time many visitors and staff at the hotel have reported seeing an apparition in room five, which they believe to have been 'Fred's' ghost. However, 'Fred' is by no means the only ghostly figure to be seen wandering through the hotel. When staying in room five, guests have heard children's voices in the next room, but there is no room next to room five! Many people also testify to seeing the ghost of a young girl wandering in the hotel's rooms and public areas. Other phenomena that have been observed by staff at the hotel's room five include a bottle of polish sliding across the room, lights flickering on and off, and taps turning themselves on and off – all without any apparent human intervention.

Location: TF8 7AL

Rope Pulling

One of the most peculiar traditions of Shropshire is the custom of rope pulling, which happened every year on Shrove Tuesday at Ludlow during the nineteenth century. On that day, at precisely four o'clock in the afternoon, a rope of particular dimensions was passed out from one of the windows in the market hall and an almighty tussle would begin between two rival camps. At its height the annual contest attracted well over 2,000 people who participated in the event

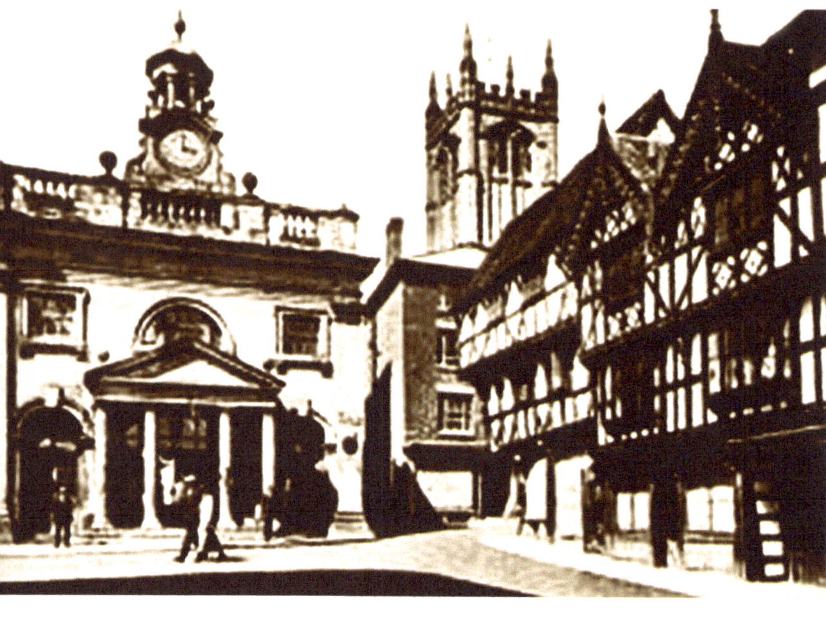

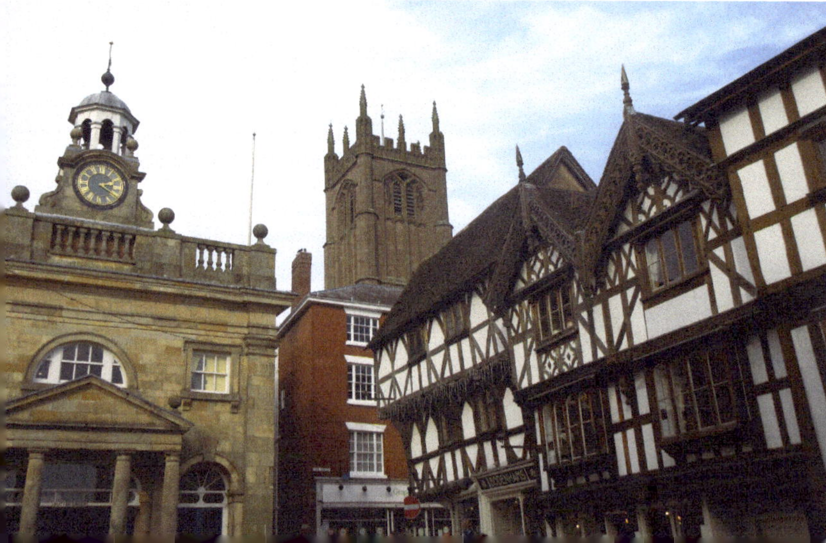

The Butter Cross at Ludlow showing the tower of St Laurence's Church and half-timbered houses.

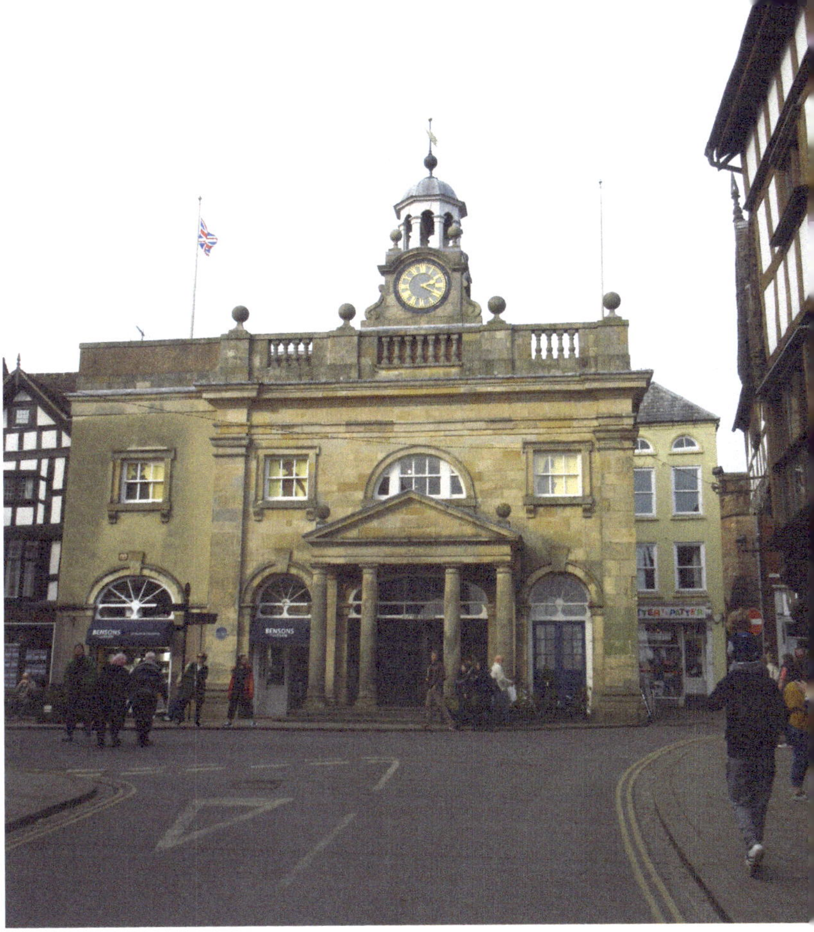

Right: The Butter Cross originally used for selling butter, milk, cheese, eggs and other dairy products.

Below: Ludlow Market today.

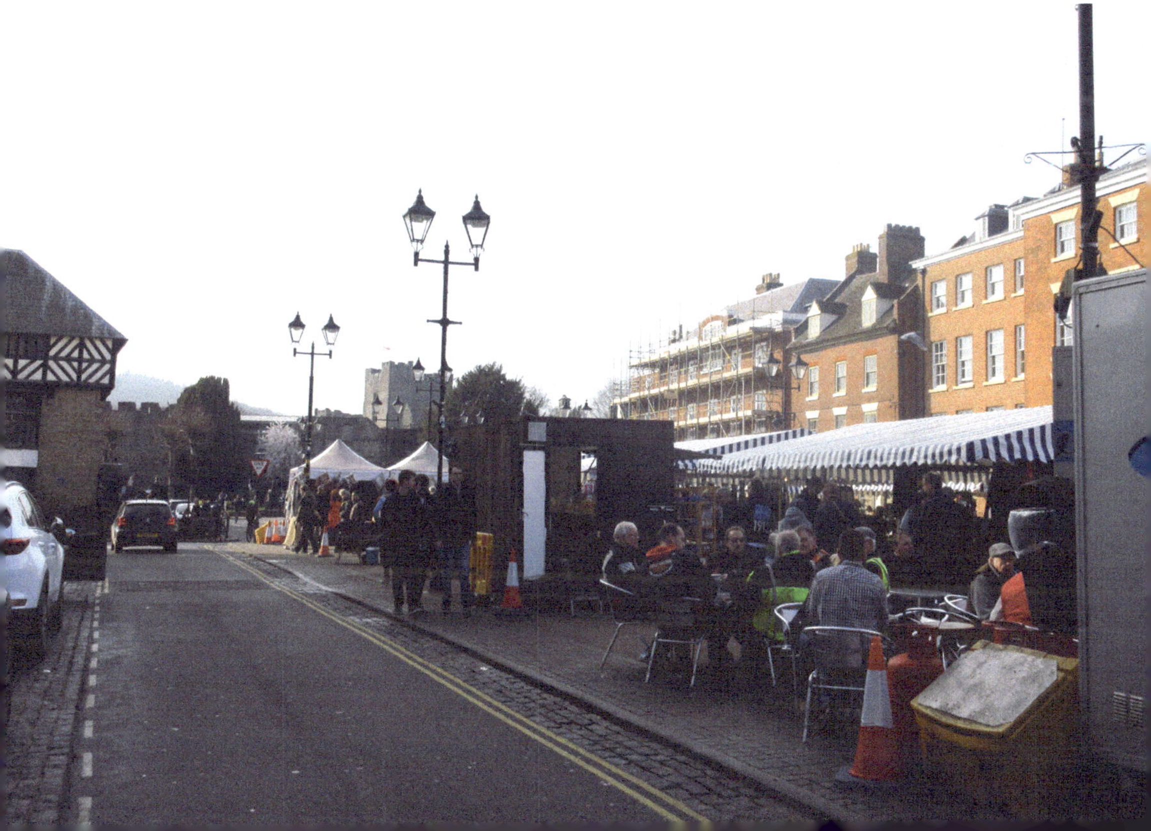

together with several more onlookers. The custom itself is said to commemorate the time of the siege of Ludlow by Henry VI, when two opposing parties arose within the town, one supporting the pretensions of the Duke of York, who was based at Ludlow, and the other wishing to give admittance to the king. One of the bailiffs, a supporter of the king, was attempting to gain entrance to the town by opening Dinham Gate, when he was barred by the opposing faction and as a result, subsequently lost his life.

As the event gained more prominence in the town, it also became more boisterous; that is until 1851 when the spectacle was curtailed. The event was revived during the 1980s when customers from two of Ludlow's pubs, the Bull and The Feathers, re-enacted the ancient custom.

However, perhaps the best account of the event was told when it was witnessed by a contributor writing to the editor of the *Every-Day Book*. Writing from Ludlow on Shrove Tuesday 7 February 1826, the correspondent observes:

> Sir,
> Among the customs peculiar to this town that of pulling a rope is not the least extraordinary. On Shrove Tuesday the corporation provide a rope three inches in thickness, and in length thirty-six yards, which is given out by a few of the members at one of the windows of the Market-hall at four o'clock; when a large body of the inhabitants, divided into two parties, (the one contending for Castle-street and Broad-street Wards, and the other for Old-street and Corve-street Wards) commence an arduous struggle; and as soon as either party gains the victory by pulling the rope beyond the prescribed limits, the pulling ceases; which is, however, always renewed by a second, and sometimes by a third contest; the rope being purchased by subscription from the victorious party, and given out again. In the end the rope is sold by the victors, and the money, which generally amounts to two pounds, or guineas, is expended in liquor. I have this day been an eye-witness to this scene of confusion; the rope was first gained by Old-street and Corve-street Wards, and secondly by Castle-street and Broad-street Wards. It is supposed, that nearly 2000 persons were actively employed on this occasion.
>
> Without doubt this singular custom is symbolical of some remarkable event, and a remnant of that ancient of visible signs, which, says a celebrated writer, "imperfectly supplies the want of letters, to perpetuate the remembrance of public or private transactions." The sign, in this instance, has survived the remembrance of the occurrence it was designed to represent, and remains a profound mystery. It has been insinuated, that the real occasion of this custom is known to the corporation, but that for the town, one supporting the pretentions of the Duke of York, and the other wishing to give admittance to the king; one of the bailiffs is said to have headed the latter party. History relates, that in this contest many lives were lost, and that the bailiff, heading his party in an attempt to open Dinham gate, fell a victim there.

Location: SY8 1AT

The Palmers' Guild

Geoffrey Baugh was a rich draper who lived in Ludlow, and 'beinge in holle mynde seying the perells of deth drawynge nyghe', decided to make his will. On the night of 12 November 1500 he sat down and made the following statement: 'to the warden of the Gylde of Our Lady and Seynet John Evangelist of Ludlow and to his Bretheryn a number of lands and tenements in and about the town of Ludlowe, of the yearly value of £3 10*s* 4*d*'. One of the properties that he bequeathed was No. 27 Bull Ring where he and his family lived. He did, however, make one stipulation in his will, and that was that 'out of the issues and yearly profits of the donated lands, the Guild should find an honest priest and singers to sing solemnly the masse of Jesus on Fridays for evermore'.

There were many other benefactors who supported the guild and its works. Indeed, for at least 300 years after 1250, the Guild of St Mary and St John, more commonly known as the Palmers' Guild, was the largest organisation in Ludlow. To attain the designation of being a Palmer, pilgrims had to show proof of their

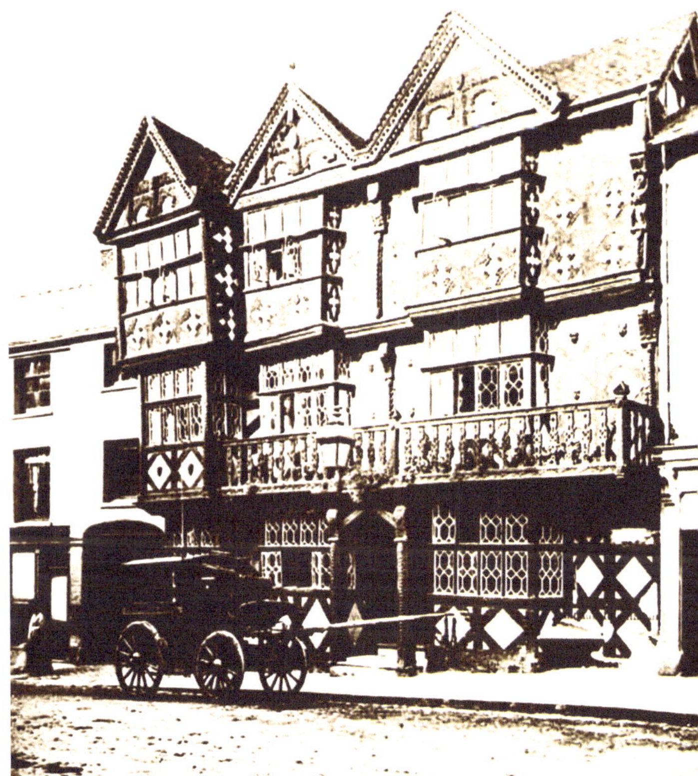

Feathers Hotel, *c.* 1899.

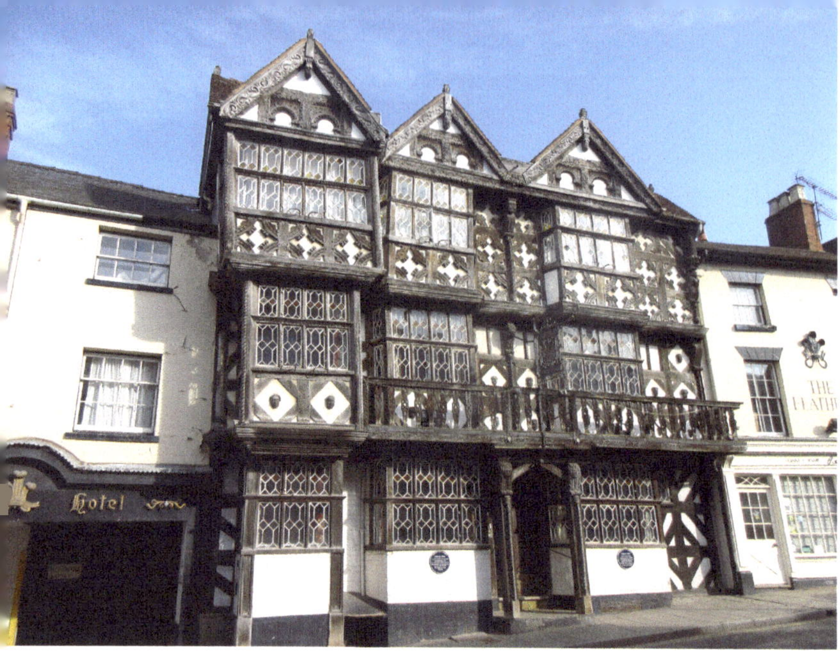

Feathers Hotel today.

pilgrimage to the Holy Land by bringing back a palm branch with them. Few actually attained this status in truth, but many wished to identify themselves with the concept of pilgrimage.

It was very expensive to be a member of the guild, which often restricted membership to the upper and middle classes. The spiritual advantage of being a member was that priests were employed who constantly said masses for the souls of members in life and after death, thus navigating a passage through the uncertainties of purgatory, and thence onwards to the sanctuary of heaven.

It was a rule of the guild that members had to be residents of Ludlow, but by the fourteenth century members were being drawn from as far as Wales, Bristol and the West Midlands, indeed from any town with whom Ludlow had trading links. There were even members of the Palmers' Guild in London. After a new

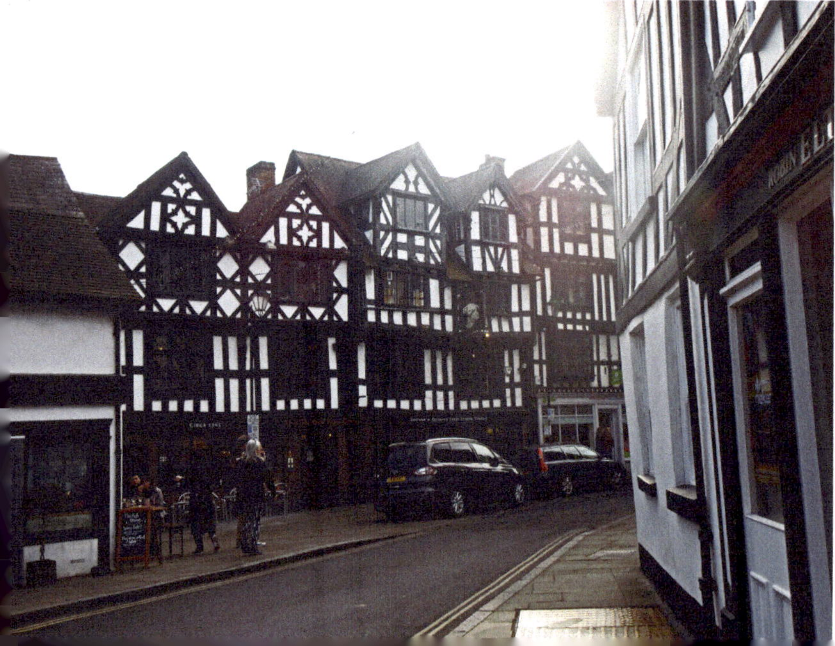

The Bull Ring today.

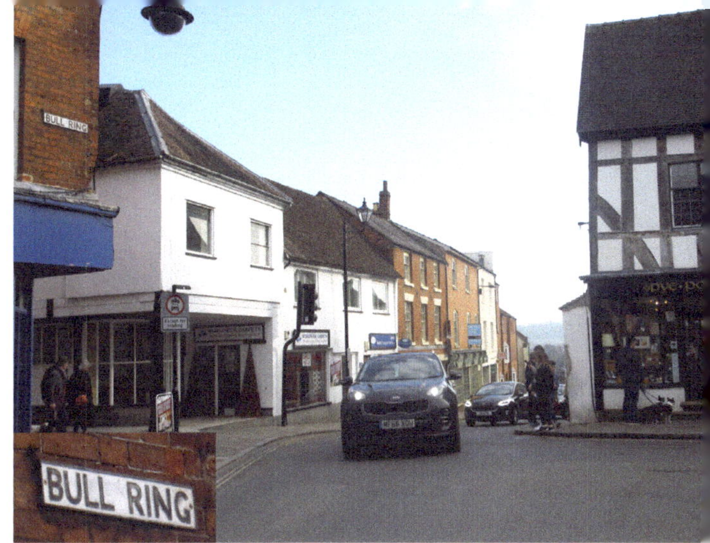

Area around the Bull Ring.

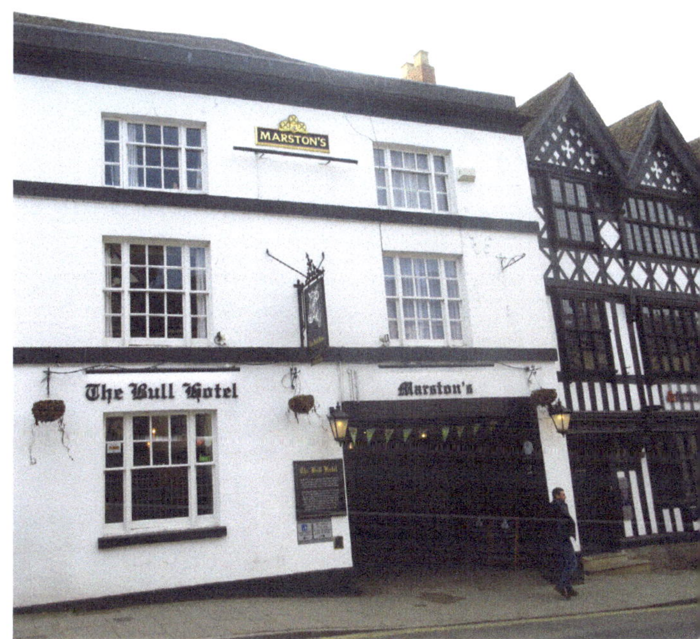

The Bull Hotel today.

residential college was built in 1394 with a communal hall and cells for up to ten priests, the role of the guild became somewhat broader, which included the management of the grammar school and the local almshouses.

The guild was dissolved in 1551 following the Dissolution of the Monasteries between 1536 and 1541 and the Abolition of the Chantries Acts of 1545 and 1547. In 1552 many of the guild's responsibilities were transferred to Ludlow Borough Corporation. By the nineteenth century, most of the guild's assets, including the estates that they owned, had been divided among the institutions they supported. However, there is still some revenue that supports the Palmers' Guild charity.

Location: SY8 1AZ

Wild Humphrey Kynaston

Overlooking the road from Oswestry to Shrewsbury, on the steepest side of Nesscliff Hill, there is a large cave known as 'Kynaston's Cave'. The cave is divided into two compartments by a wall of rock and can be approached via a flight of steps. The cave was once the dwelling place of the convicted murderer Humphrey Kynaston. Not only did he rob the rich to give to the poor, but it was alleged that he sold himself to the devil.

Humphrey Kynaston, or 'Wild Humphrey' as he was more normally called, was the younger son of Sir Roger Kynaston of Hordley the castle keeper of Middle Castle and Knocking. After his father's death Humphrey became tenant of the castle. However, because of his riotous manner of living he soon found himself deep in debt. Then, on 20 December 1491 Kynaston was found guilty of the murder of John Hughes at Stretton. He was forced to leave the castle and seek shelter in a cave near to Nesscliff Hill – the cave is still known as Kynaston's Cave.

It is said that 'Wild Humphrey' had a magnificent horse that was always shod backwards, the intention being to make it impossible to track him. Many people believed that the steed was in fact the devil himself in the shape of a horse. This belief was reinforced when one day, when being pursued by constables, Kynaston leaped from the top of Nesscliff Hill to Ellesmere, a distance of at least 9 miles. Others suggested that the leap was from Nesscliff to Loton Park – a distance of at least 5 miles – and thence to the top of the Breidden Hill. Everyone who believed

Lane leading to Wild Humphrey's Cave.

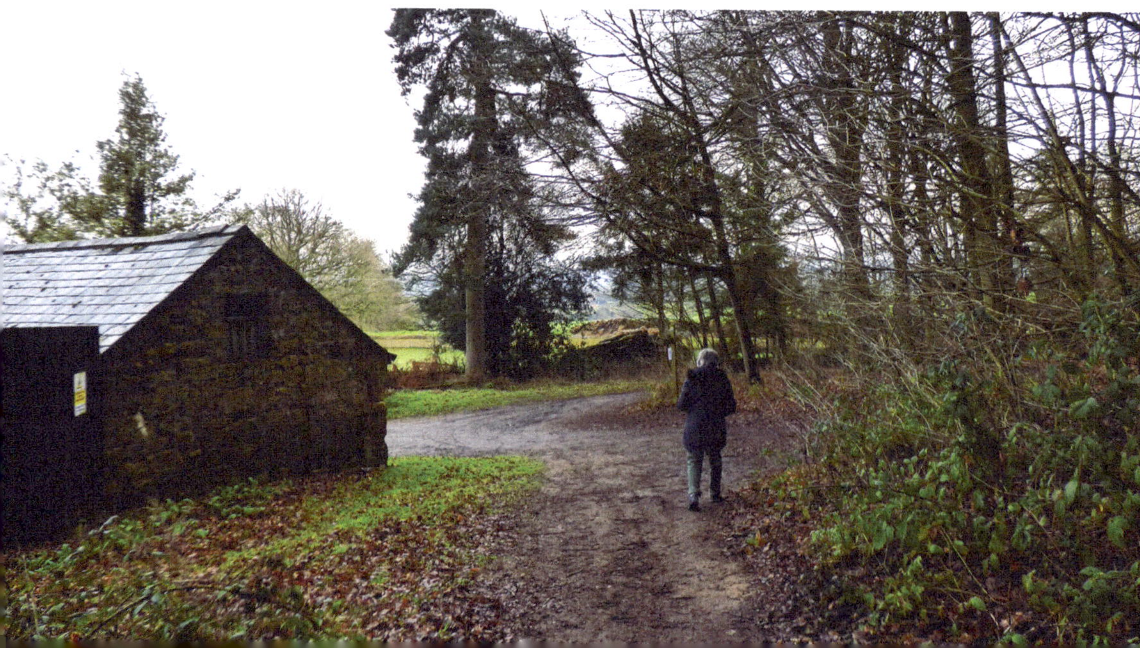

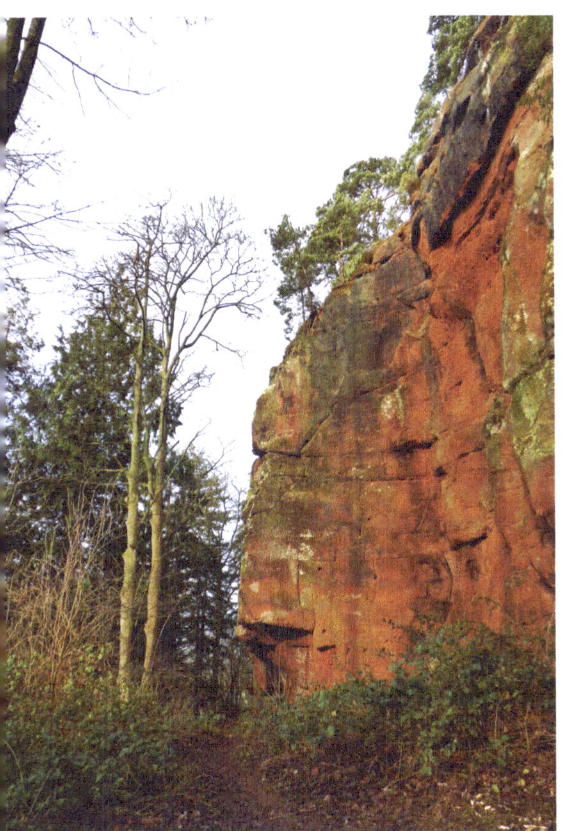

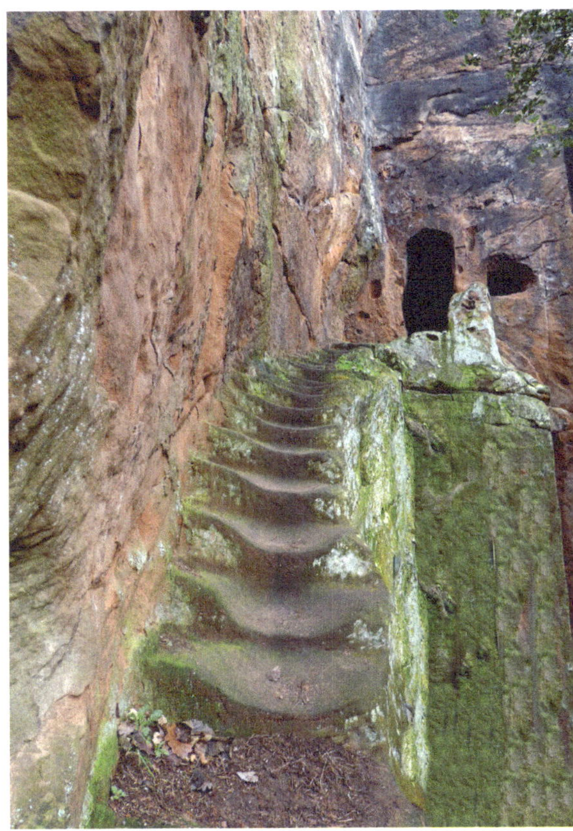

Above left: Access path to Wild Humphrey's Cave.

Above right: Entrance to Wild Humphrey's Cave.

the story also believed that he could not have achieved such a feat without the intervention of the devil himself. It is said that the horses hoof marks can still be seen on the banks of the River Severn at a place that is still known as 'Kynaston's Leap', for it was here, according to legend, that he had crossed over Montford's Bridge, ending up on the Shrewsbury side of the river. Unbeknown to Humphrey, the undersheriff came with a large company of men to the wooden bridge and removed several of the planks, thus preventing his return. They then laid in wait. When Humphrey returned later in the day, he sensed the trap and, galloping towards the bridge, he leapt over the width of the river, which was about 40 feet wide at that point, thus avoiding being taken prisoner.

On another occasion Humphrey rode into the courtyard of Aston Hall and demanded refreshment. He was brought ale, which he then proceeded to drink without dismounting. While he was drinking the hall's gates were closed, and preparations were made to seize him. However, upon finishing his drink, Humphrey pocketed the silver tankard, leapt over the assembled company, over the closed gates and out into freedom!

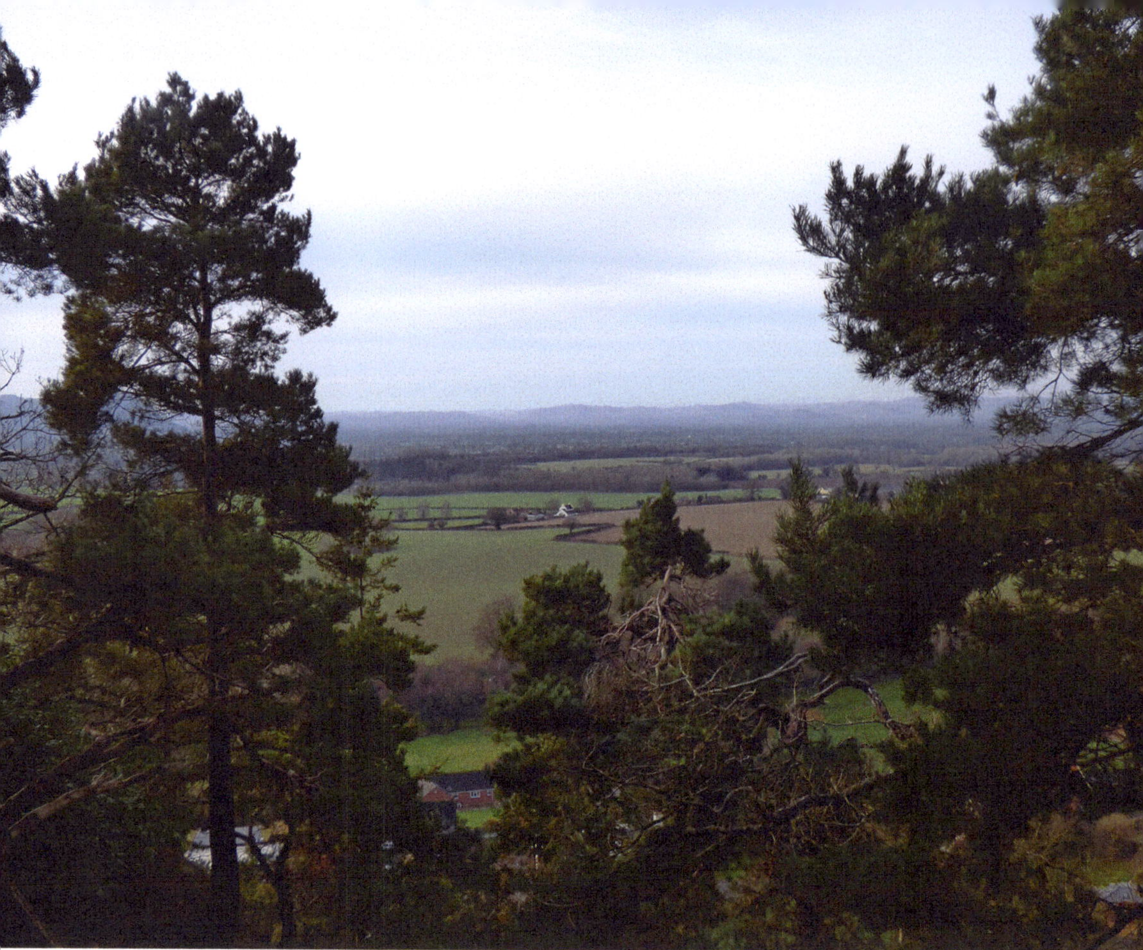

View from Wild Humphrey's Cave.

Humphrey's constant companion, his horse, lived in the adjacent chamber in the cave. Days were filled with audacious exploits, save for Sunday, when his mother journeyed over from Ruyton to bring him his dinner.

Wild Humphrey was a champion of the poor. Another tale is told that when one day he saw two carts on the road, one with three horses and the other with one; he immediately took off the leader from the first, and fastened it in front of the single horse, making them equal. He was loved by the people, who cooked many of his meals and fed his horse. It was undoubtedly their friendship, together with his own cunning and ingenuity, that saved him from capture. Wild Humphrey died peacefully in his cave.

Location: SY4 1DH

The Legend of Revd Carr

After leaving his vicarage in Woolstaston, the rector, Revd Edmund Donald Carr, would lead the Sunday morning service in the little church. Then, after lunch, he would set off to conduct the afternoon service on the other side of the hills at the church in Ratlinghope. This ritual continued for more than ten years, during which time the rector never once missed leading the service. Even in the heavy winter snow, the rector made his weekly journey across the hills, never once losing his way, but, walking over the Long Mynd was not without its difficulties, especially when there was low cloud over the tops.

On a particularly cold winter's Sunday in 1865, when the ground was covered with a thick carpet of snow – the worst snow for over fifty years – Revd Carr thought that he might not be able to get over to see his parishioners

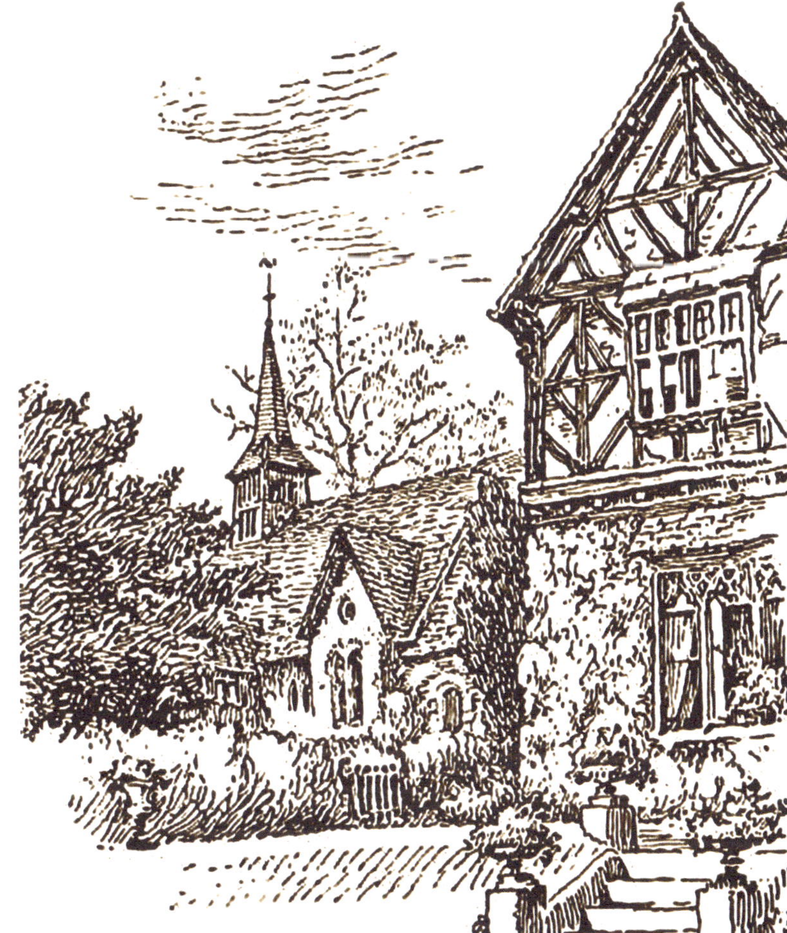

Sketch of the Church of St Michael and All Angels, Woolstanton.

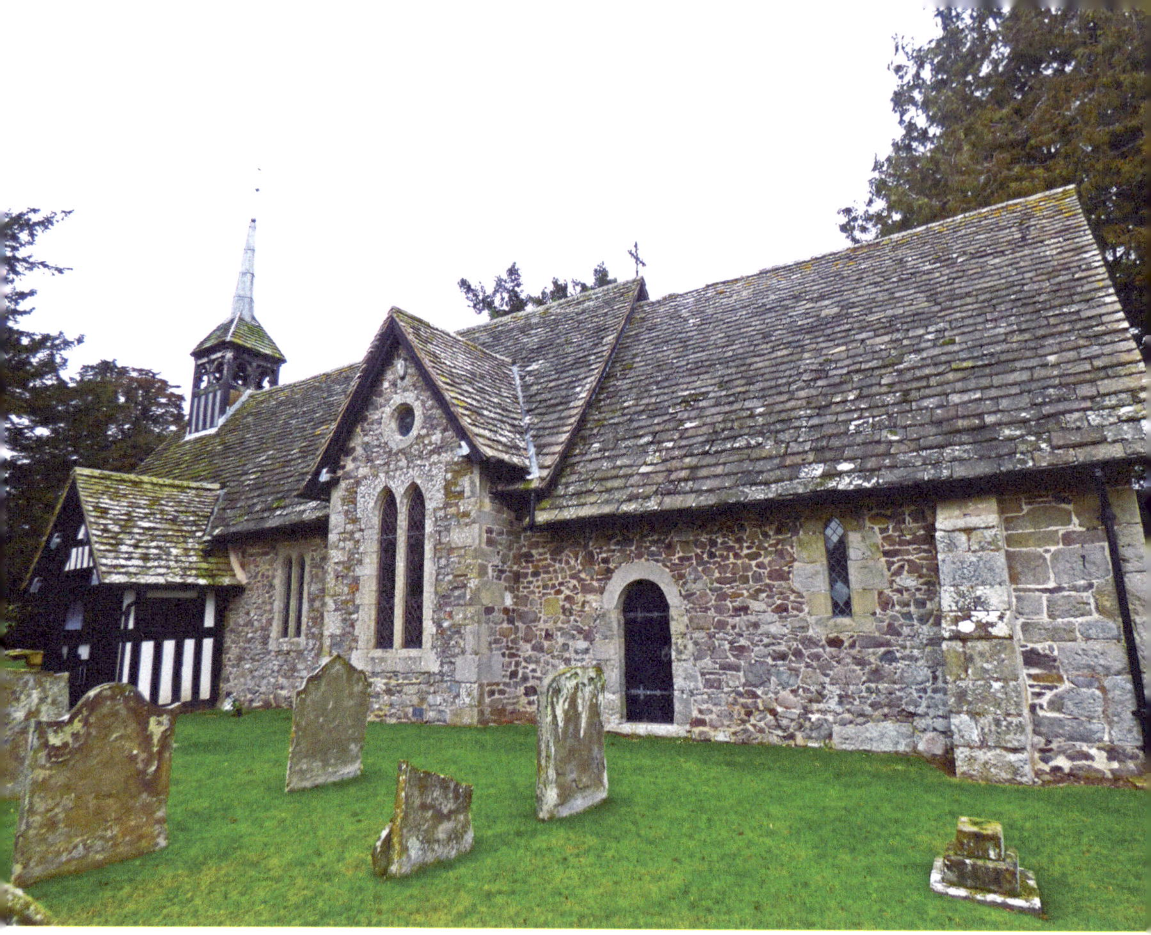

Above: Church of St Michael and All Angels, Woolstanton.

Below: Rectory of St Michael and All Angels, Woolstanton, as it looks today.

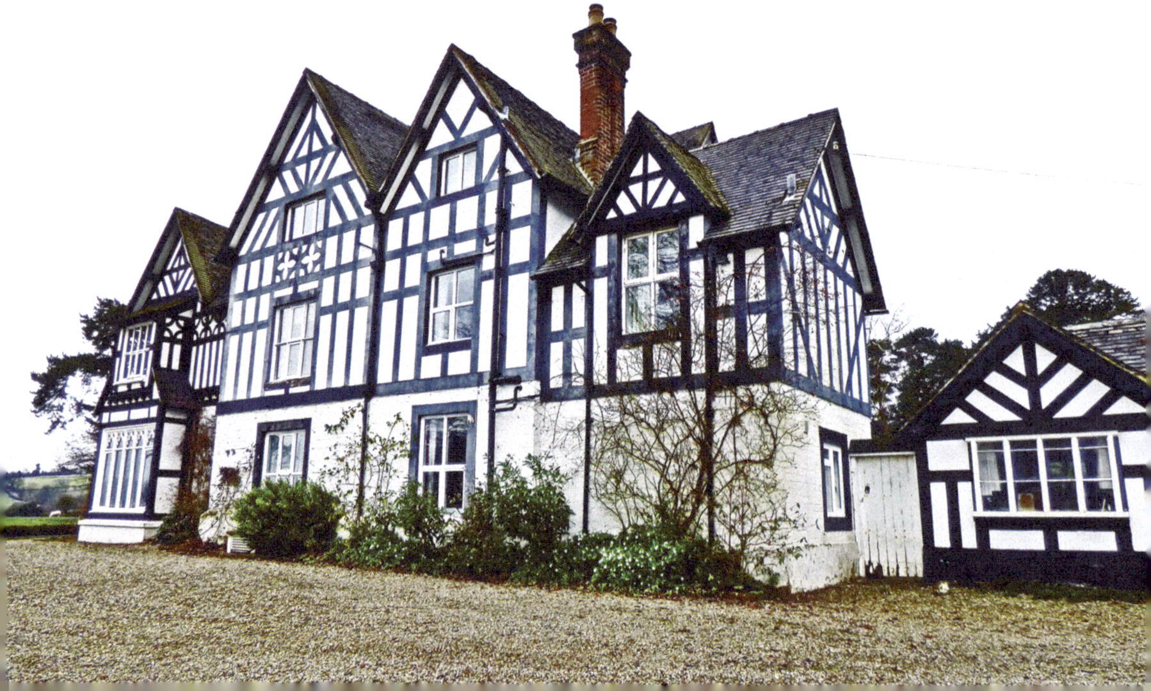

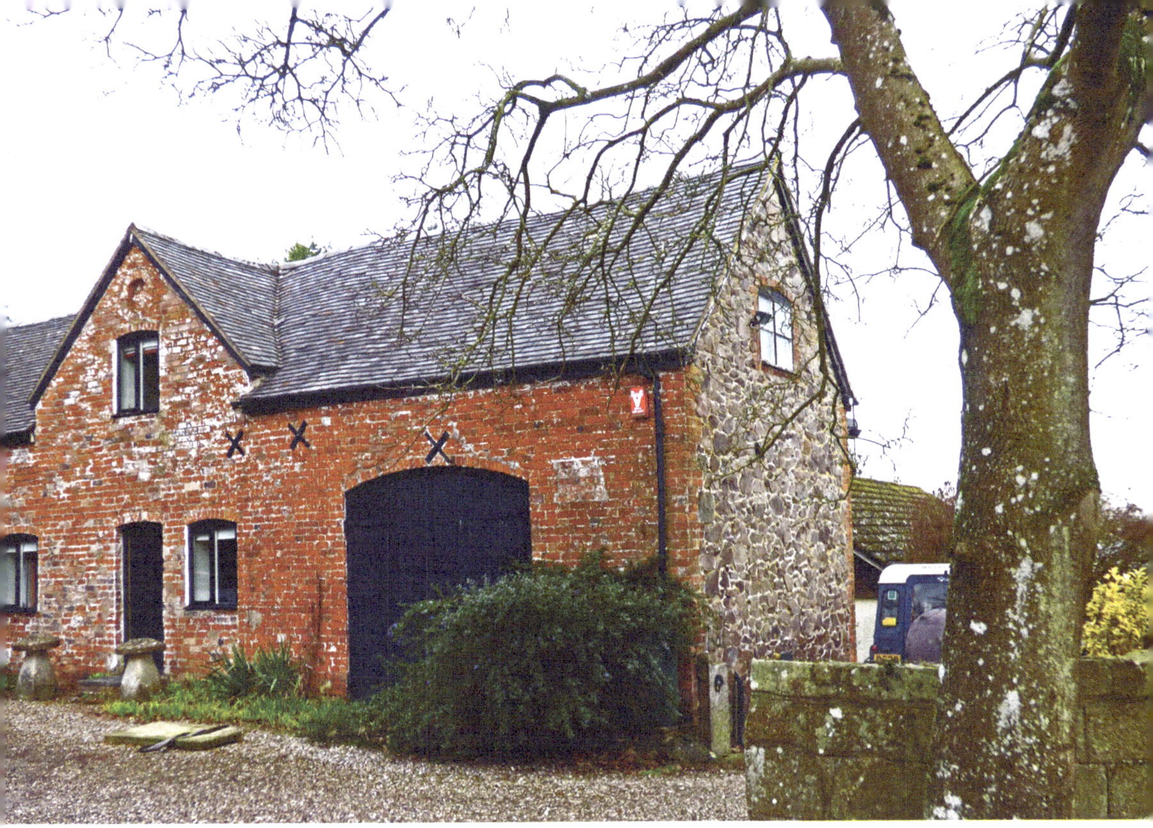

Above: Original stables at the Church of St Michael and All Angels, Woolstanton.

Right: Headstones of Revd Carr and his wife, Elizabeth, in the graveyard of St Michael and All Angels.

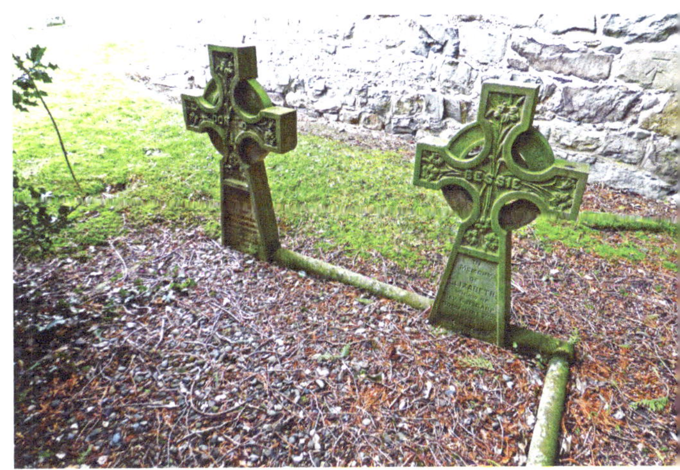

in Ratlinghope. However, he decided that he would at least attempt to make the journey. After leading the service at Woolstaston his servant saddled two horses and they set off for Ratlinghope. They'd travelled less than a mile when the rector decided to send the servant back to the vicarage, saying that he would continue on foot. It was obvious that the horses couldn't cope with the deep snow drifts.

Struggling on, the rector sometimes found himself up to his thighs in snow, and on more than one occasion he had to crawl on his hands and knees. After de-icing his clothes a few times and taking a number of well-earned rests on the 4-mile journey, he did eventually reach the tiny hamlet of Ratlinghope.

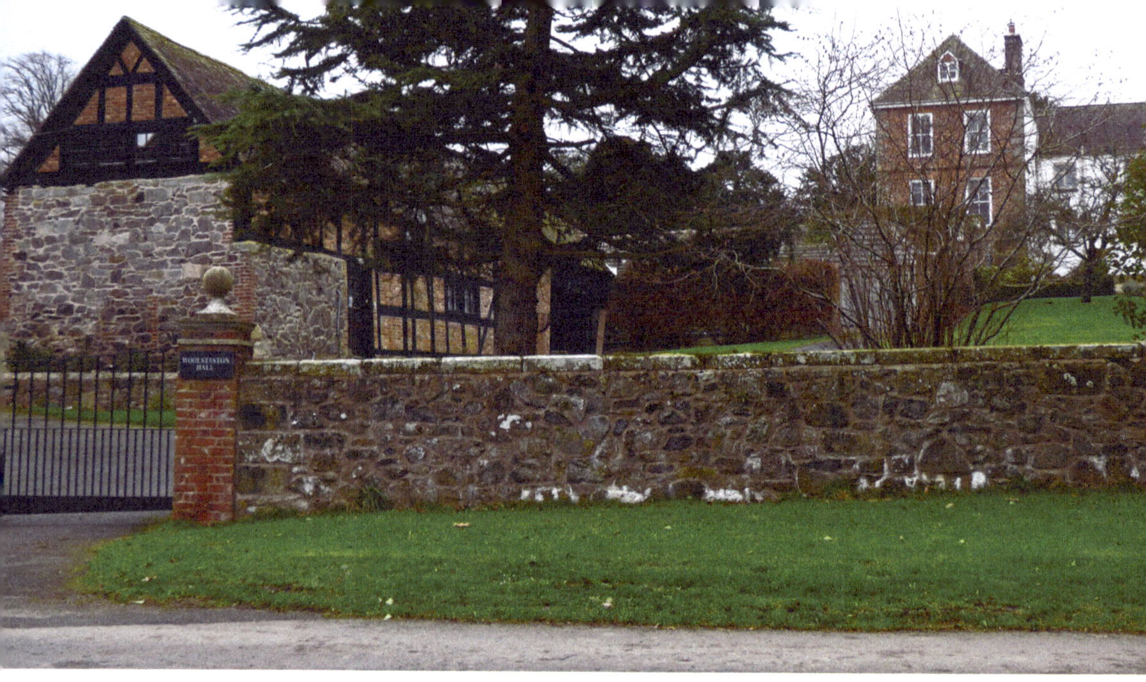

Woolstaston Hall today.

The few parishioners who attended the service were more than surprised to see him and begged him to stay overnight, but he declined the offer, saying that, apart from anything else, he had to return to lead evensong at Woolstaston Hall.

As Revd Carr was climbing out of the village a great storm blew up, but he continued on his journey, endeavouring to keep to his route. At length he came to a slope that was unfamiliar to him, and, seconds later, he found himself sliding down the side of the Long Batch. Although he tried to break the fall, he was powerless to stop himself from careering into the rocks below. Digging his heals into the snow, he eventually came to a halt just before reaching the rocks. When he did manage to stand up, he realised that he was completely lost, the snow was even deeper than it had been earlier, he was hungry, and it was going very cold as night was drawing in. His plight became even worse when he fell again, losing his hat and gloves.

As morning approached, he could still not tell where he was. He also realised that during the long night he had become snow-blind. Collecting his remaining energy and senses together, Revd Carr then heard a flowing stream, which he proceeded to follow down, and although he didn't know it at the time, it was the stream above Light Spout Hollow, and what the good rector was unaware of was the fact that rather than proceeding along the path of the stream, he was in fact encircling the waterfall. Then, just when he was thinking that the situation could not become any worse, he actually lost his boots!

Lying in a deep snowdrift the rector thought that his earthly life was fast drawing to a close when he heard the sound of children playing in the snow. He managed to raise his head, and was recognised by one of the children. They helped him to a nearby cottage before he was taken to be examined by a doctor. After a long period of recuperation at home, the rector eventually made a full recovery.

Location: SY6 6JG

Some Old Funeral Customs in Shropshire

The choice of flowers to adorn coffins in Shropshire has always been a subject of much discussion. Women at Baschurch never agreed as to the proper flowers to be used for the purpose; some preferred everlasting flowers, whereas others had a preference for wallflowers, while still others favoured roses. Conversely, Edgmond folk preferred to be guided by the seasons for their choice of funereal flowers.

In former times in Shropshire, even domestic creatures shared in the family's grieving. Bees were gently told of the death in the household, and rooks were also warned. At Church Stretton the farm horses were given the day off, and at Ludlow many townsfolk believed that even the fowls hid away until after the time of the funeral.

Similarly, the choice of pall-bearers was a matter of great importance. It was always the tradition that this sad office was performed by the deceased close friends and neighbours. On Wenlock Edge the choice of pall-bearers was also a matter of great significance, and if anyone near to death had forgotten to address this matter, they were soon reminded of their duty by friends and family. The rules that were normally followed were very simple: aged or married people were borne to the grave by married men, young men were carried by their male friends, and girls and unmarried women were carried by young women. However, if the distance to carry the coffin was great, or if the coffin was very heavy, then the coffin would be carried for most of the way by young men. In the case of the death of infants and little children, it was normal practice for married women to carry the casket, or young girls dressed in white dresses or boys wearing white scarves.

It was not unheard of for people to make preparations for their own funerals well before the appointed day. One old lady in Bedstone, sensing that the end was near, kept her own coffin in her cottage, so that everything would be prepared when the day came.

There was an unusual funeral tradition observed in the area around Edgmond and Market Drayton. Whenever there were female bearers at a funeral, they were accustomed to wearing a peculiar garment called a 'funeral hood'. The hood was made of a single width of plain white muslin and was around 3 yards in length and a yard or more wide. The hood was pleated at the top and fitted over the wearers head. The remaining length of muslin fell down on each side, shrouding the wearer in the ample folds, forming a cloak and hood in one; no doubt a strange sight for people coming from outside of the county.

There was another unique burial custom in Edgmond, and that was the tradition of 'ringing the dead home.' In this ritual, all of the church bells were rung – instead of just one bell – while the funeral party made its way to the church. Just before reaching the church a minute bell was tolled. The bells signified the welcoming of the dead to their last resting place.

The 'passing bell' was still rung in the parish churches of Shrewsbury up until 1879. As soon as the church clock struck ten on the night after a death, the sexton would toll the bell seventy times, to signify the 'threescore years and ten' of human life.

Location: TF10 8JW and throughout Shropshire

The Lion Hotel

John Ashby, a former mayor and town clerk of Shrewsbury, was the man who had The Lion on Wyle Cop built in the 1770s. Earlier, sometime in the sixteenth century, there was an inn called The Red Lion on the site. Ashby invested vast sums of capital in the project, but not enough it would appear, as he was declared bankrupt. When he died in 1779, some of the contents of the hotel needed to be sold to pay off the debts that he had incurred. The hotel lease was taken the following year by Robert Lawrence, who had a sound business plan and soon transformed the place into one of the most successful coaching inns in the region.

Perhaps the most famous coach to call at The Lion was 'The Shrewsbury Wonder'. 'The Wonder', with its distinctive yellow livery, made an early start from London, leaving at 6.30 in the morning and, after stopping for a short while in Birmingham, arriving at The Lion at 10.30 later that night – a truly remarkable journey when the state of the roads and the distances involved are taken into account.

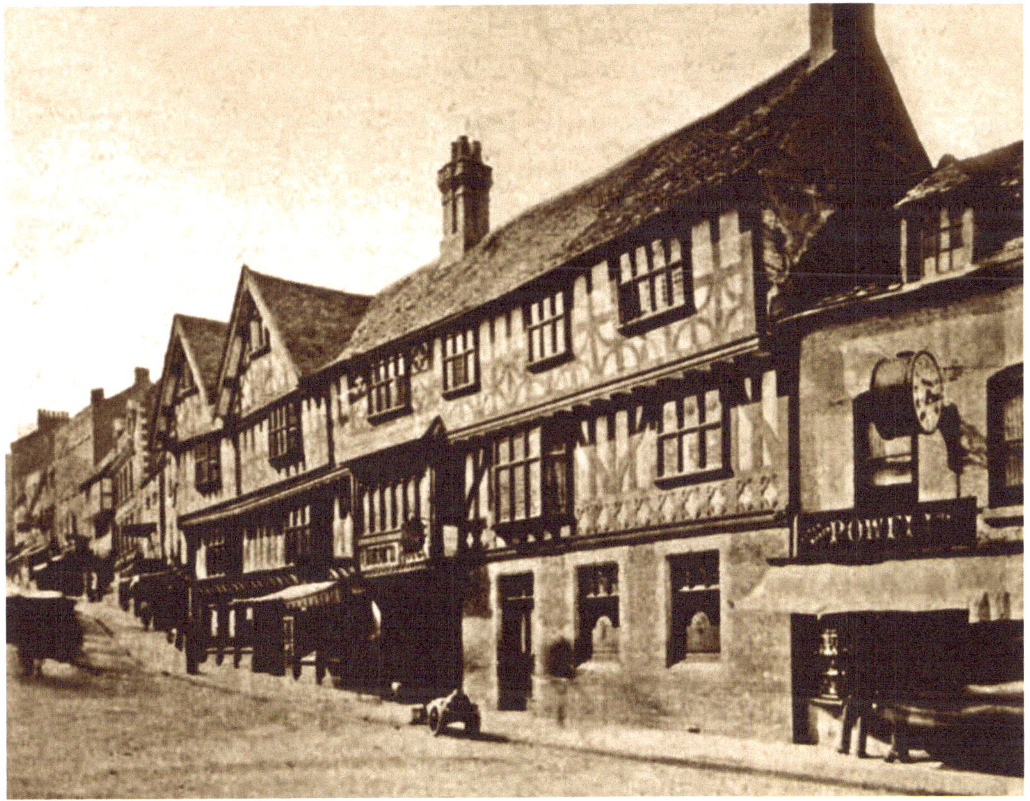

Wyle Cop, Shrewsbury, in the nineteenth century.

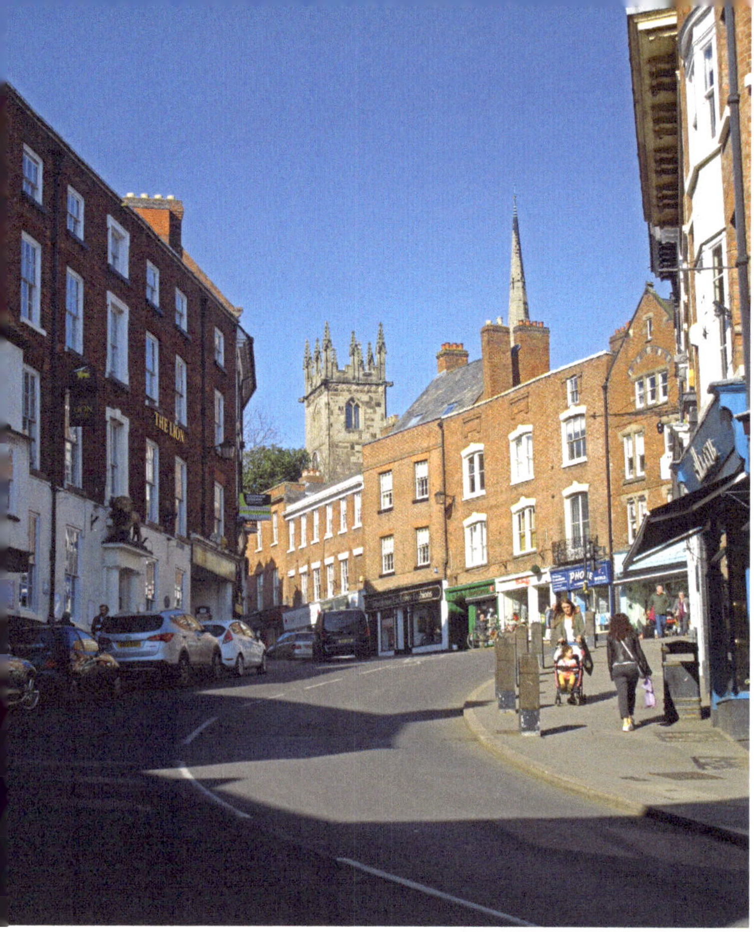

Left: Wyle Cop today.

Below: The Lion Hotel today.

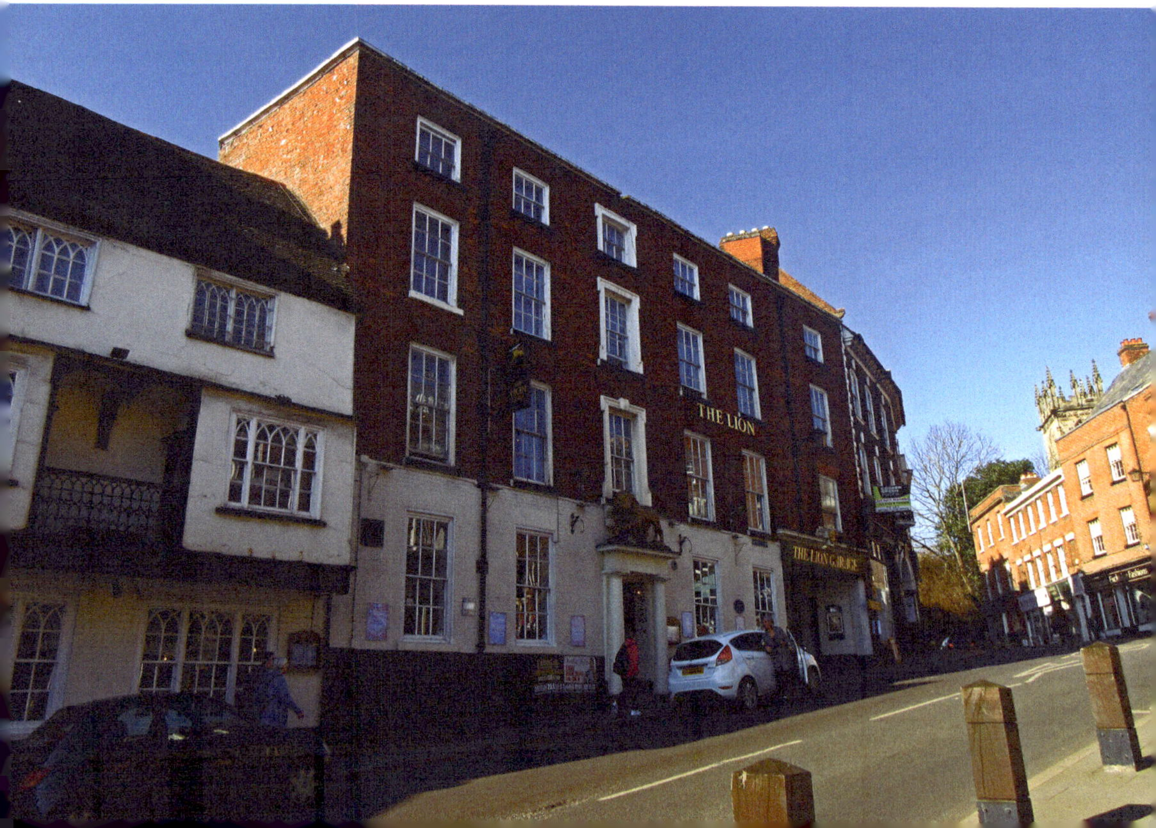

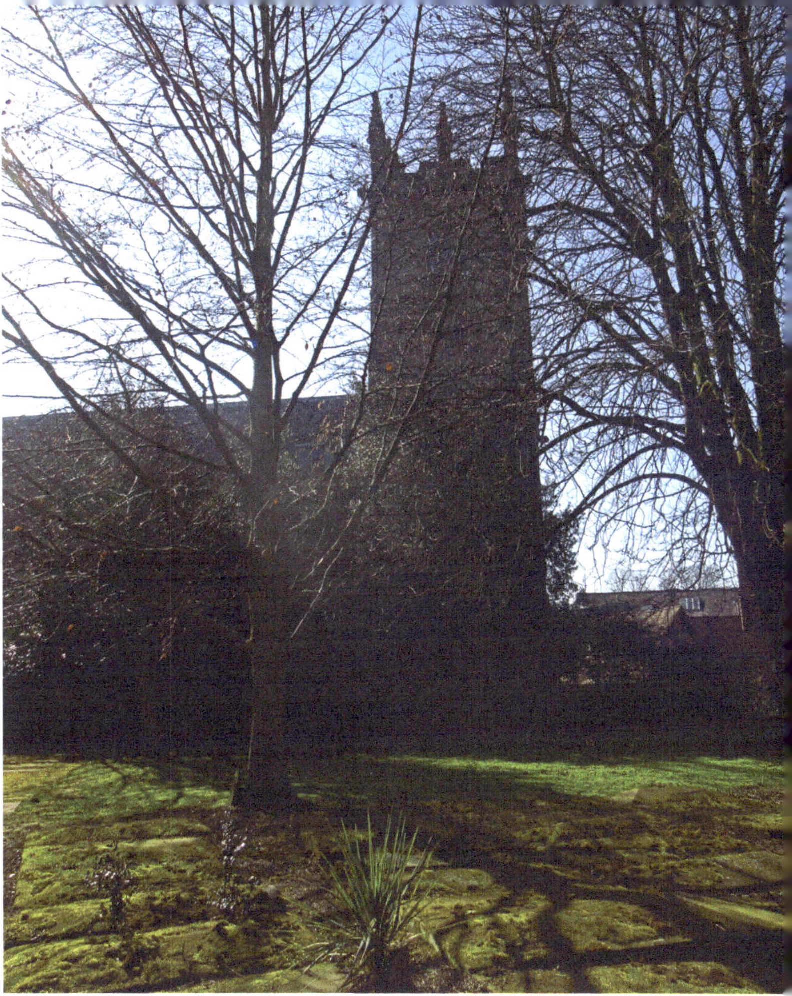

Graveyard at St Julian's where Sam Hayward, coach driver of 'The Shrewsbury Wonder', is buried.

Over the years many famous guests have stayed at The Lion, including Niccolò Paganini, Benjamin Disraeli, Charles Dickens and Charles Darwin among others, but maybe one of the most well-remembered guests was a gentleman who was staying at the hotel during the 1800s. When he didn't come down for breakfast one morning it was assumed that he was lying in, but this was not the case! The gruesome truth was revealed later in the morning, when staff found that he had died in his room. With all due respect his body was taken to the nearby church where a short service of committal was held before he was buried. However, the tale doesn't end there. Later in the day, the gravedigger thought that he heard screams coming from somewhere in the churchyard, but he didn't investigate any further, and continued with his work. However, the screams became more intense, and the gravedigger soon realised that they were coming from the grave he had dug earlier that day. Without further ado he set about reopening the grave and coffin, where he soon found to his horror that the man had been buried alive, and had actually died within his own coffin. As if to prove the point, there were several scratch marks on the underside of the lid of the coffin where he had tried to free himself.

Location: SY1 1UY

Hide and Seek

Flowing for 220 miles from its source in the Welsh Cambrian mountains, the River Severn is the longest river in Britain. The name 'Severn' itself is a derivation of Sabrina (Hafren in Welsh) and is 'lifted' from the mythical story of Sabrina, a nymph who drowned in the river. It would seem that since time began, the River Severn has played a significant part in the life of the county of Shropshire, and in the various towns through which it flows, none more so than the market town of Bridgnorth. The river has been a source of economic wealth for the town, but it has also caused disruption and chaos during flooding, a fact sadly known to the parents of two young children.

In the 1600s the two children of Magpie House, Charlotte and William, were playing a game of hide and seek in the cellar of the house when they were inadvertently locked in. The cellar of the house was close to the River Severn, which was in full flood at the time. When the river suddenly burst its banks and flooded the cellar they were left with no means of escape. As the waters in the cellar steadily rose around them, they cried for help, but their endeavours were all to no avail. Holding hands, they died together in the flooded cellar.

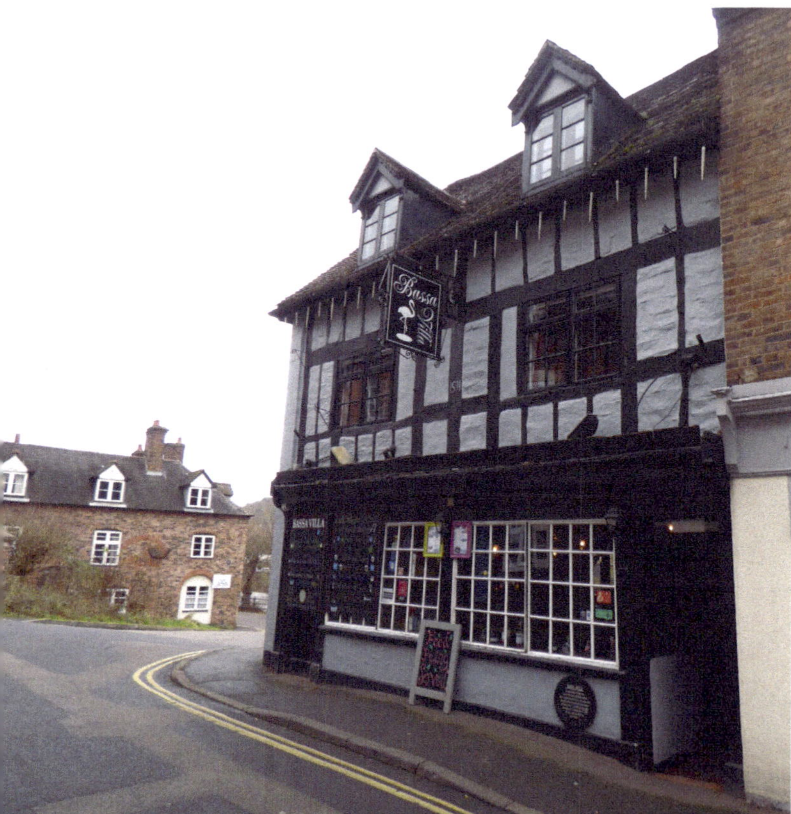

Bassa Villa.

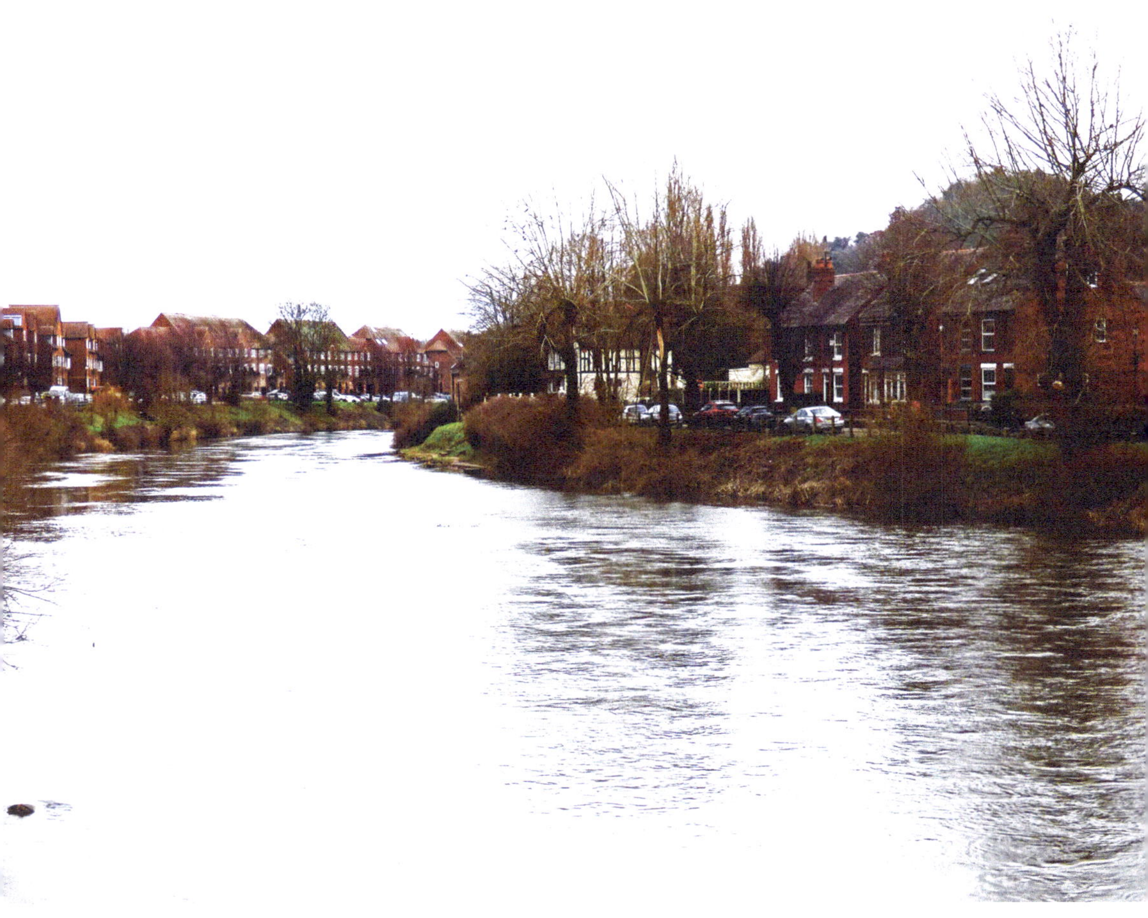

River Severn near to Bassa Villa.

Their inconsolable and remorseful parents found it almost impossible to come to terms with their burdensome grief. Although never again able to see their children happy and lively, they nevertheless wanted some lasting memorial to commemorate their short lives. They commissioned two marble images to be made, which they had placed in the Terrace Gardens.

A more recent discovery threw new light on the story. A 10-inch-diameter hole was found in the floor of the pub's cellar. Further investigations indicated that the void was indeed the mouth of a well. Speculation was rife as to whether the children actually died in the cellar as a result of the banks of the river bursting and flooding the cellar or whether they drowned in the well – but speculation is all that can ever be! Although the well must have been there for as long as the building itself, there is no specific record relating to it, and it is not shown on the sewerage plans that date from the 1850s. Some consideration has, however, been given as to whether the well was used as a source of water in the Castle Gate Brewery.

The history of the restaurant that is now known as the Bassa Villa goes back a couple of centuries. Starting as the Beehive, the pub was located at No. 17 Cartway, Bridgnorth. Sometime later the pub moved to different premises at No. 82 Friars Street. Finally, the business was transferred to Nos 47 and 48 Cartway. Following this change of address, the pub became known as The Magpie in around 1780.

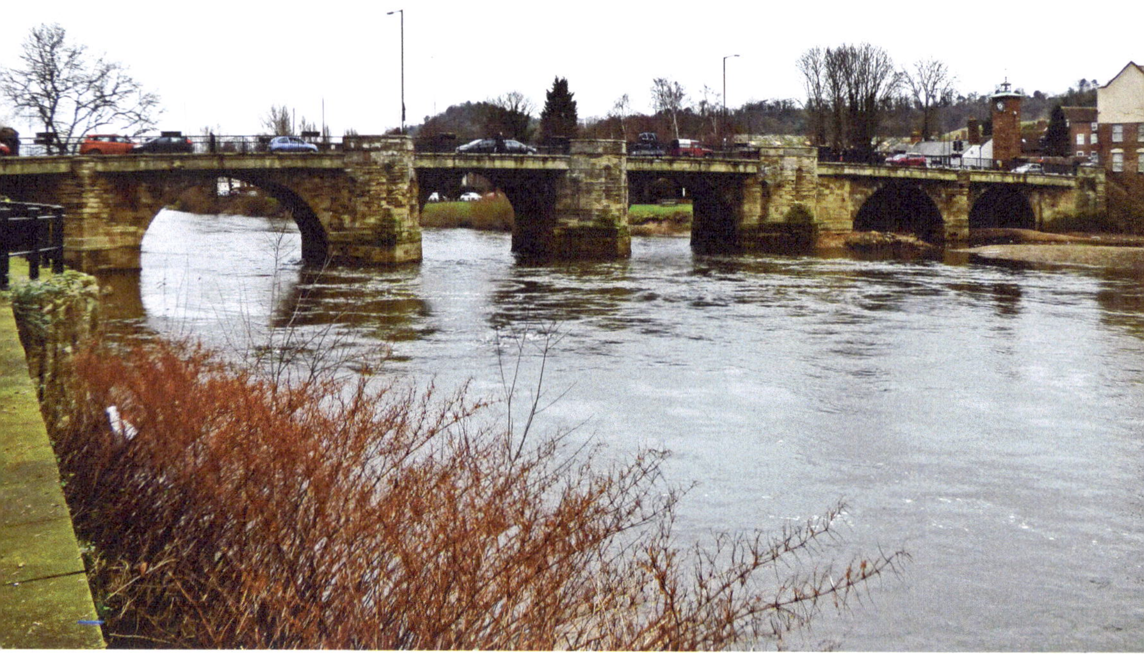

Bridgnorth Bridge over the Severn.

During those far-off days, not only was the pub famous or infamous for allowing Sunday drinking, which was illegal at the time, it also boasted having a secret escape tunnel from the stables to the river.

There is a plaque in the restaurant that declares a mother's undying love for her two dead children, being victims of a tragic accident following the playing on an innocent children's game.

Managers, both past and present, have experienced strange happenings while working in the cellar, and at what appears to be random intervals, a middle-aged lady dressed in black, who, known as the Lady in Black, has been seen by both staff and customers, wandering throughout the pub, sobbing tearfully, a bereft and mournful expression on her face, as she continues her relentless search for her two lost children. On other occasions she has been seen to have had a smile on her face, no doubt bringing to mind the happier times that she enjoyed with them. Even now, people visiting the pub often hear strange noises whenever they inadvertently go anywhere near the cellar.

Location: WV16 4BG

Hannah Phillips of Astley Abbotts

Entering the Church of St Calixtus in the Shropshire hamlet of Astley Abbotts, the remnants of the funeral of Hannah Phillips can be seen. Her 'Maiden's Garland', symbolising purity, still hangs on an iron rod with its heart-shaped frame holding the gloves that she would have worn at her wedding. The inscription on the garland declares that Hannah Phillips was unfortunately drowned while crossing the River Severn a day or two before her wedding.

Hannah's family lived on the far side of the River Severn and, more often than not, they crossed by using a ford at a particularly shallow stretch in the river. On the eve of her wedding, 10 May 1707, Hannah made her way to the church to

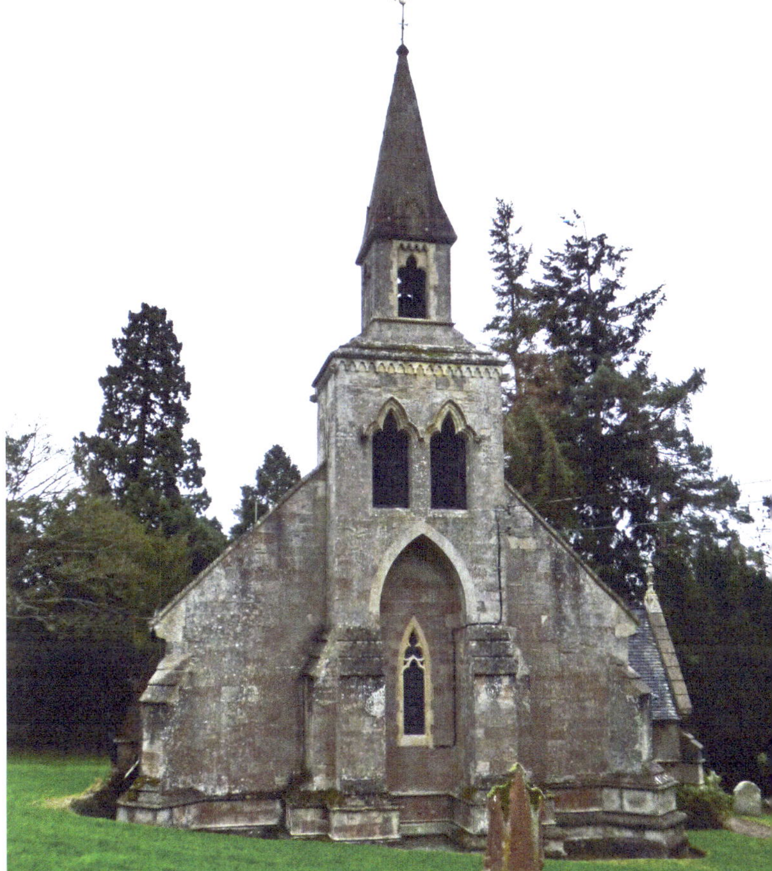

Church of St Calixtus, Astley Abbotts.

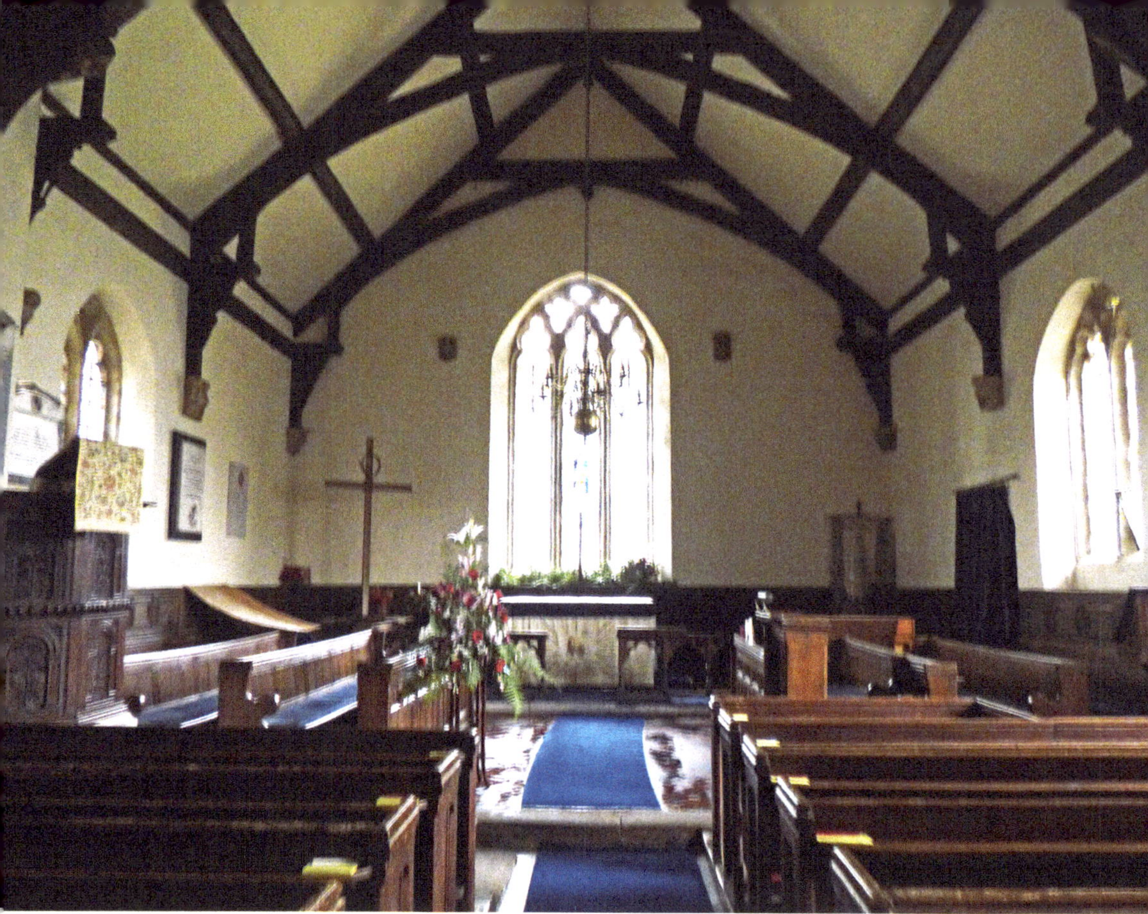

Interior of St Calixtus, Astley Abbotts.

help with the preparations. It is thought that she might either have crossed by the ford or if the river had have been swollen, then she would have used the nearby ferry. But, one way or another, she was never seen alive again. Many local people believe that she slipped at the ford and drowned, and that her body came to rest in a sunken cave below the ford. Sometime later her small clutch bag was found floating in a pool a little further downstream.

The memory of the tragedy of Hannah Phillips's death only remained with her family and close friends, until, that is, the early part of twentieth century. It was then that a local resident was returning home one evening when, somewhere between Severn Hall and The Boldings, he saw a young woman appear from out of a nearby hedge, but when he braked to avoid her, she completely disappeared. From the description he gave at the time, it would seem that she stood a little over 5 feet tall and was dressed in a long skirt reaching to the ground. She also wore a shawl draped around her head. Later, when recounting this event to a close neighbour, he was informed that the young woman, who he confirmed was very slim and appeared to be dressed in clothes from an earlier age, was, in all probability, the ghost of Hannah Phillips on her way to church.

Many years later another resident had a similar experience. He was cycling home after finishing his work when, at the same spot as the previous witness, he

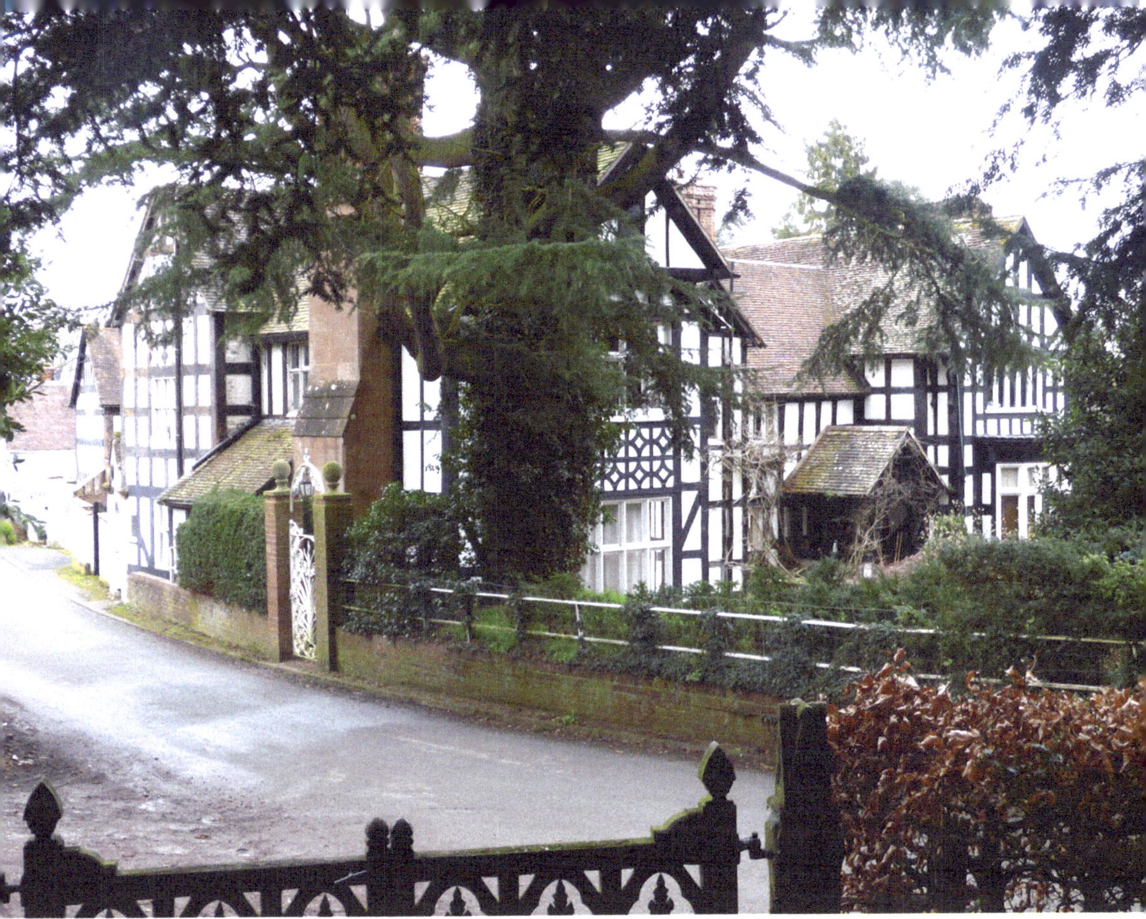

Main road through Astley Abbotts.

saw a young man suddenly appear. As he drew closer, the young man, who was dressed in a dark brown suit with breeches, disappeared into the evening mist. It was suggested that this apparition could have been Hannah Phillips's intended husband, still out looking for her.

The practice of displaying a 'Maiden's Garland' at the funeral of an unmarried woman or girl is an ancient custom, dating, it is believed, from the time of the Romans. The symbolism proclaims virginity and innocence. During the funeral, the garland is carried by two young girls dressed in white and having folded handkerchiefs on their heads. They lead the funeral procession into the church, and then place the crown, as the garland is often called, on the coffin where it resides until the body is committed to the earth. At the end of the service, the garland might be placed in the grave of the maiden, hung in the chancel or placed over the pew that the young girl's family occupied. Sometimes the crown is hung in a convenient place in the church, such that everyone entering will pass beneath it. Custom then dictates that if the presence of the crown in the church remains unchallenged for a given number of weeks, then it is hung from the ceiling with a record of the date and the name of the deceased.

Location: WV16 4SW

The Haunted Hotel in Market Drayton

Market Drayton is a small market town in Shropshire, close to the Welsh and Staffordshire borders. Lying between Shrewsbury and Stoke-on-Trent on the River Tern, the town was formerly known as Drayton in Hales and prior to that Drayton. A charter for a weekly Wednesday market was granted in 1245 by Henry III, which led to the town's name being changed to Market Drayton. The town's weekly market is still held on Wednesday.

The Corbett Arms Hotel is a famous seventeenth-century coaching house, which, prior to 1825, was called The Talbot.

Old Corbet Arms Inn, Market Drayton.

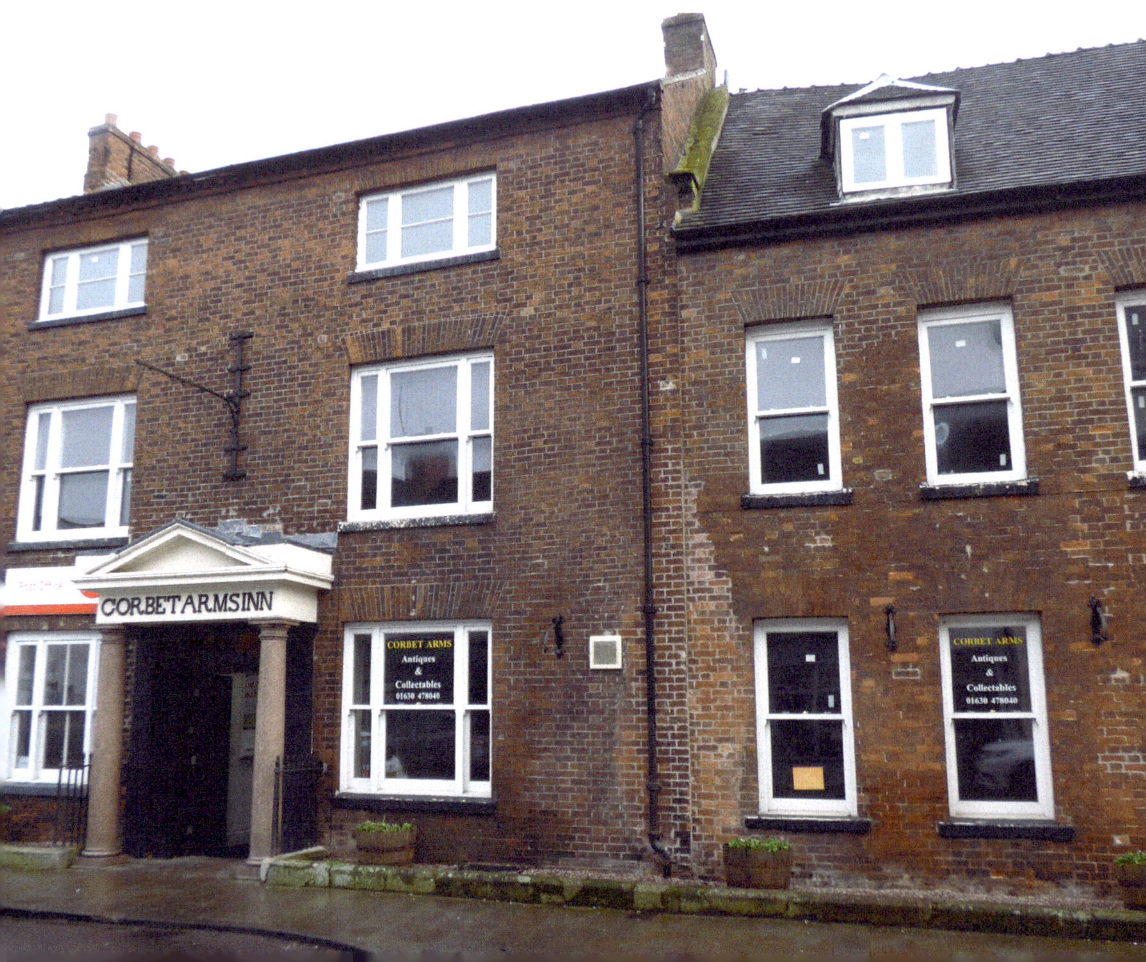

During the construction of the Shropshire Union Canal, Thomas Telford used The Corbett Arms Hotel as a base from which he could monitor progress.

However, our tale concerns a dapper and very handsome travelling salesman who, from time to time, was wont to stay at the hotel. On one such visit a young and impressionable chambermaid became infatuated with the beguiling guest. He, being more worldly-wise and all too aware of the maid's body language, took full advantage of her naive and youthful innocence. Before long they were enjoying a passionate and intense illicit affair that she had willingly consented to on the promise of marriage, a promise that he'd no doubt made to other chambermaids in other hostelries up and down the country. Their illicit affair was conducted in room 7 of the hotel, the room that he invariably stayed in when visiting the town. The inevitable happened, and the chambermaid found that she was pregnant with his child. She was not, however, unduly perturbed, as she recalled that he had made a promise to marry her. She went to break the news to him, only to find that he had left the hotel that very morning without leaving any forwarding address. She was distraught on hearing this, being all too aware of the ensuing consequences.

Rather than be thrown out destitute onto the streets, she decided to take her own life. She was found hanging by the neck from a hook in the rafters of room 7. Ominously, the hook still remains! From that time onwards her ghost has been seen on the stairs at the back of the hotel – stairs that are believed to have been used by the hotel's staff – and, whenever there is a young bachelor staying in room 7, it is often the case that all of the bedclothes are ripped off the bed during the night as she continues her quest to find her errant lover. Guests have also reported that items of jewellery have gone missing, only to be found in a completely different location.

The Corbett Arms Hotel has now been converted into a post office.

Location: TF9 1PY

Old Mo's Ghost

A community of Franciscan monks, or Grey Friars as they were known because of the colour of their habits, lived in the Bridgnorth Friary on a strip of land on the banks of the River Severn. The history of the friary is fragmented, but it is known that the order was founded in the town sometime between 1224, when the Franciscans first came to England, and 1244 when Henry III made a payment to the friars to help towards the building of their church. Later, at the time of the Dissolution of the Monasteries between 1536 and 1541 – the friary being surrendered on 5 August 1538 – an inventory was made by the King's Commissioner, making reference to the quire, the belfry, the kitchen, the brewhouse and the refectory. It is known that there was also a dormitory and a chapter house. During the dissolution all of the friary's silver was taken, the bells were melted down and sold, and even the lead from the friary roof was taken and sold. At length, the remaining buildings were converted into a malthouse.

There is a tale allegedly relating to a 'fallen' friar known as Old Mo who at one time lived in the friary. Renouncing his holy vows, Old Mo took to drink

River Severn near to the site of Bridgnorth Friary.

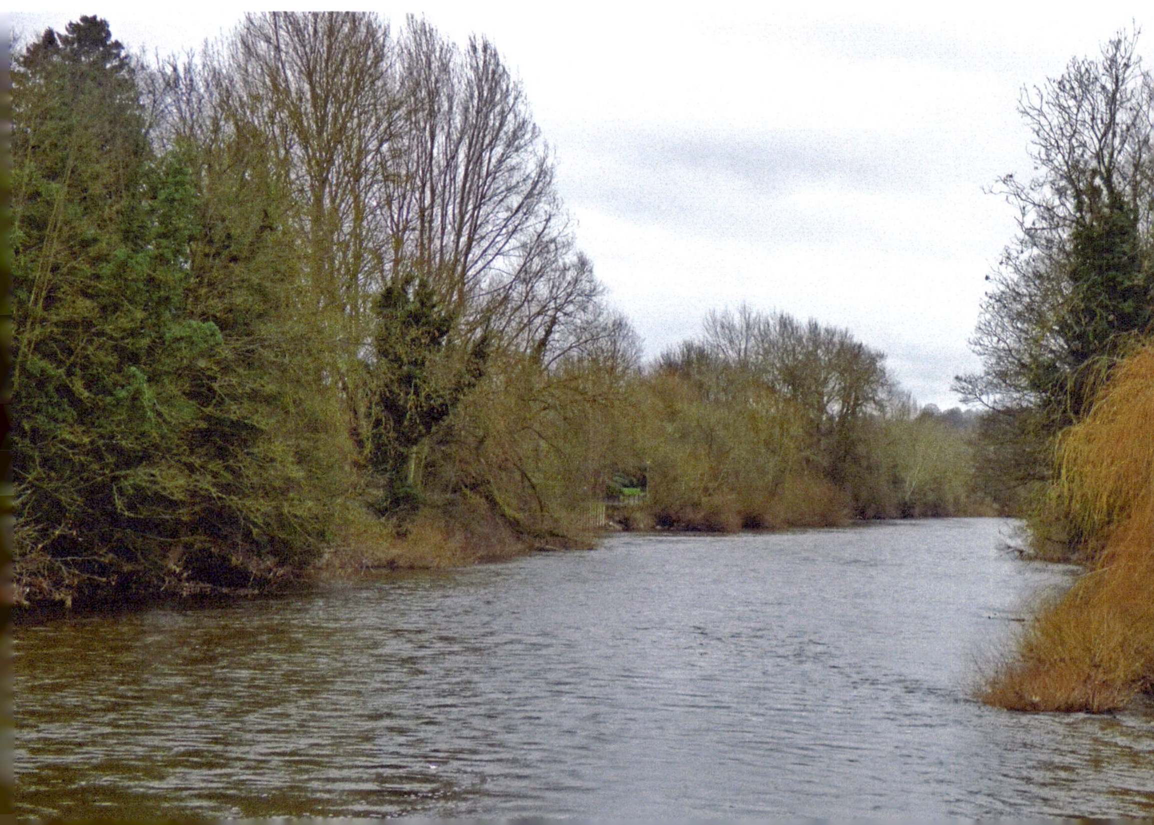

and debauchery. His favourite haunt was known as Old Mo's Alley, which ran from Love Lane and then on to Bramble Ridge. Tired of putting up with his shenanigans, the monks became totally exasperated, so, after he'd enjoyed a riotous night out, a small group of friars confronted him on his way back to the friary. They accosted him and tried to reason with him, but all to no avail. Unfortunately, when reasoning failed, the altercation turned nasty and Old Mo ended up dead after being beaten and poisoned. His body was then disposed of, but nobody knows whether he was buried in the grounds of the friary or dumped in the river.

Many years later the company of Southwell & Co. was founded by Joseph Southwell, who first came to Bridgnorth as a carpet weaver in 1809. The Southwell carpet factory was built on the site of the old Franciscan friary between 1824 and 1826 by Thomas Martin Southwell, and the company was formally established in 1828. As the factory buildings were extended a number of artefacts from the friary's cemetery were uncovered, and it was not unusual for workmen to find coffins and, on occasions, human skeletons. When further extensions were being made to the carpet factory in 1887 two more skeletons were found. During the Second World War, when the site was being used by the Rootes Group to build parts for aeroplane engines, many people claimed to have seen Old Mo dressed in his grey habit. Later, when the factory was once again being used by Southwell's, many others testified to seeing the ghost of Old Mo.

The carpet factory, having come to the end of its natural life, was demolished in May 1989, making way for new housing on the riverside. During the demolition and subsequent building more human remains were found.

Location: WV16 4DS

The Bloodstained Hand

From Anglo-Saxon times until the sixteenth century, Condover Manor was at various times an estate belonging to the Crown. Then, in 1586 the estate was either given to or bought by Thomas Owen, a Member of Parliament and Recorder of Shrewsbury. Local legend declared that Owen's father was an ostler at the Lion Inn at Shrewsbury, but in truth he was the eldest son of a Shrewsbury merchant, and was educated at Oxford University gaining a BA in 1559. Three years later he entered Lincoln's Inn and was called to the Bar in 1570. In addition to being a Member of Parliament he was also a member of the Council in the Marches of Wales and a Justice of the Common Pleas.

However, before Thomas Owen owned the estate, Condover Hall had been the scene of a heinous crime. Lord Knyvett, the then lord of the estate, had been murdered. His butler, John Viam, was accused of the murder, largely on the evidence given by Sir Harry Knyvett, Lord Knyvett's son. During the trial, Knyvett had sworn under oath that Viam had stabbed his father to death. Having been found guilty of the crime, Viam made the following declaration immediately before facing the gallows: 'Before heaven I am innocent, though my master's son swears me guilty. And as I perish an innocent man, may those who follow my murdered lord be cursed.'

Being obsessed with justice, Owen remained unconvinced as to the outcome of Viam's trial. He spent many hours studying the trial records and concluded that there had been a gross miscarriage of justice, believing that the true murderer was Knyvett's own son, Sir Harry Knyvett.

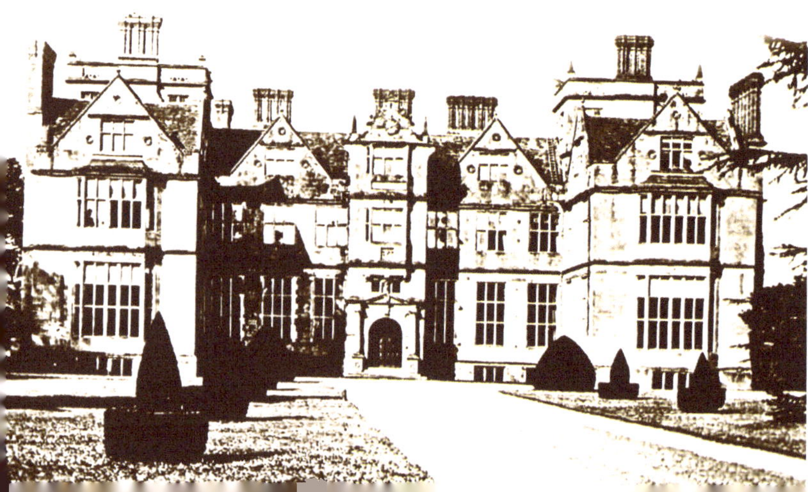

Front entrance to Condover Hall.

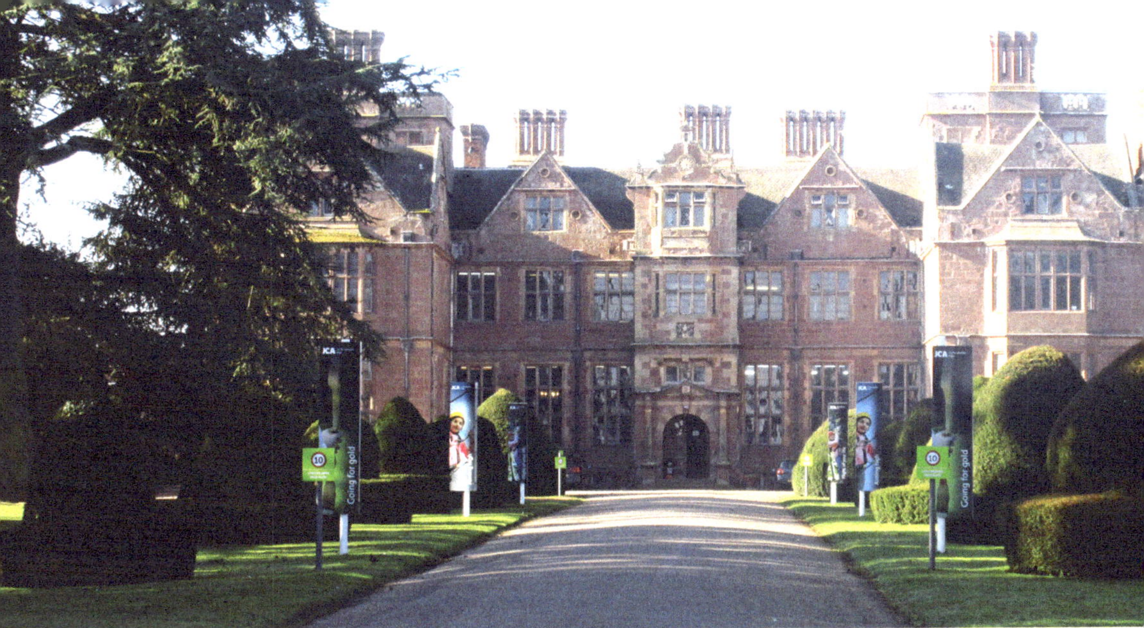

Condover Hall today.

Owen was held in high esteem by Queen Elizabeth, and because of this she took the unusual step of granting a retrial. Owen himself led the prosecution, although some accounts suggest that he was the trial judge. The trial was scheduled to be held in Shrewsbury but fearing that there was the possibility of public order offences being committed, Owen begged another favour of the queen. In order to divert attention from the trial, the queen consented to visit the town to watch a play being performed by the boys of Shrewsbury School. In the event the trial was concluded before the queen had arrived at Shrewsbury. A coded message was sent to her at Coventry and she returned to London. During the trial itself it was proved beyond reasonable doubt that Knyvett had murdered his father by stabbing him near to the top of the stairs to the basement in the hall. Then, in his attempt to escape from his son he stumbled down the stairs, placing his blood-covered hand on the staircase wall for support. For many years afterwards the imprint of the bloodied hand could not be washed away, and was eventually removed when the stone was chipped clean. Knyvett, who since his father's death had become Lord of Condover, was hanged.

According to legend Elizabeth I granted Condover estate to Thomas Owen because of his efforts in bringing Knyvett to trial, but the truth is a little different from that. In 1586 Owen actually purchased the estate and Condover Hall from the Vynars, who had previously owned the estate.

It is certainly the case that since the unjust conviction and death of John Viam, owners of Condover Hall have been subjected to chequered fortunes. Indeed, it is still believed locally that Viam's curse is still cast on the hall.

In more recent times the sound of footsteps has been heard near to the entrance to the Hall's basement, while others claim to have seen two ghost-like figures wandering through the hall dressed in Victorian clothing.

Location: SY5 7AU

Bishop's Castle

When Egwen Shakehead was miraculously cured of palsy at the shrine of St Ethelbert sometime before the Norman Conquest, he gave as an offering the Manor of Lydbury to the Church of Hereford – an estate of some 18,000 acres. The Bishop of Hereford then built Bishop's Castle sometime before 1078 with the stated objective of guarding the Episcopal Manor of Lydbury from the attentions of the Welsh. At the time of building, the castle was known as Lydbury Castle.

Sometime in 1263 when Prince Edward was at Shrewsbury, he wrote to his father and asked him to instruct Bishop Agneblame to reside in the Castle of Lydbury North for security reasons, but when the king arrived in Hereford the following year, he found that the bishop was still absent from his diocese. A strongly worded letter was immediately despatched to him, threatening to take back into royal hands all of the lands that had been bestowed to the diocese.

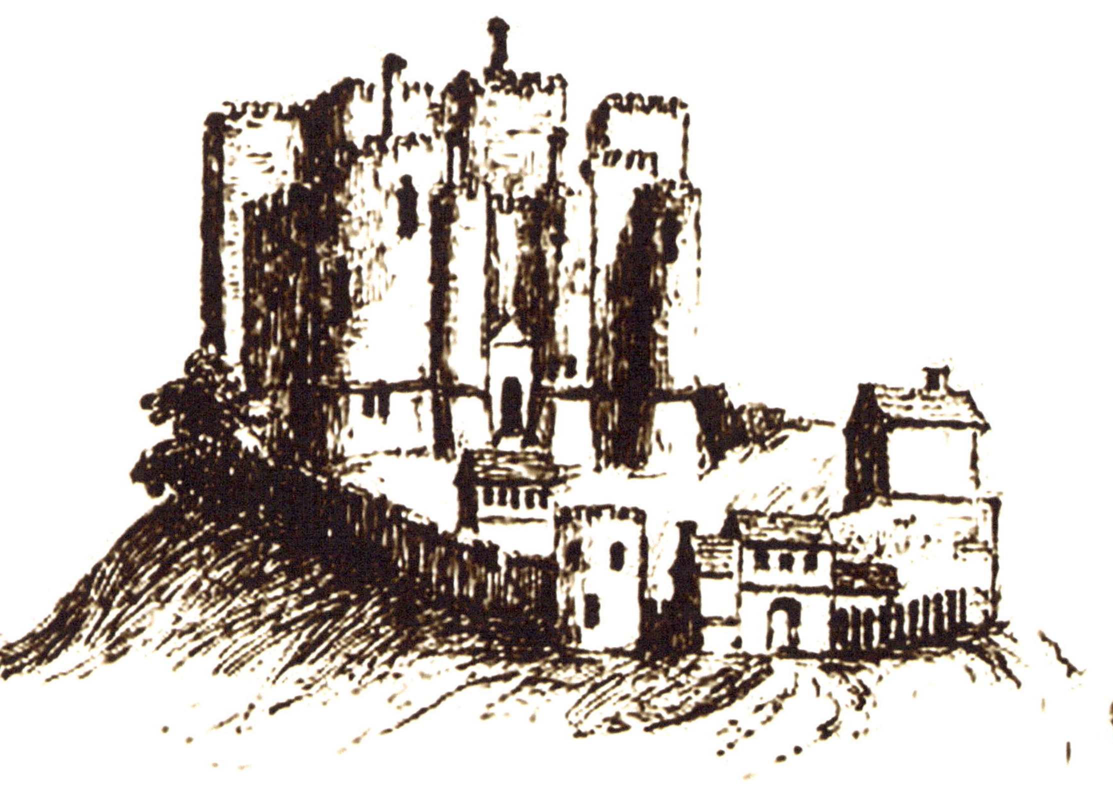

Sketch of Bishop's Castle.

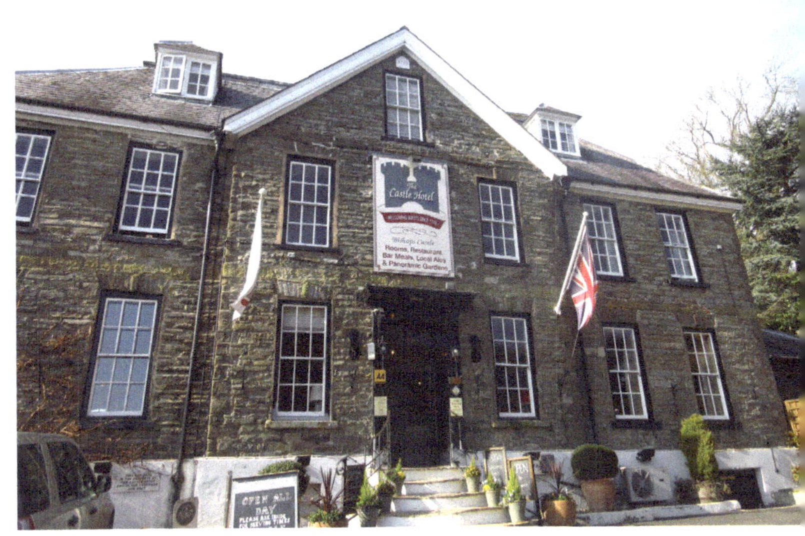

The Castle Hotel, Bishop's Castle.

The bishop returned with alacrity, only to fall into the hands of the neighbouring barons, who, during his absence, had joined in the insurrection of Simon de Montfort. The bishop was taken prisoner in his own cathedral and subsequently held in the Castle of Eardisland.

It would appear that there was good reason for the bishop to absent himself for, 'on the Thursday next after the Transfiguration of the Blessed St. Thomas the Martyr, in the 47th year of King Henry III, Sir John Fitz Alan, Lord of Arundel coming to Bishop's Castle, took there the said Castle; and the constable was treacherously slain'.

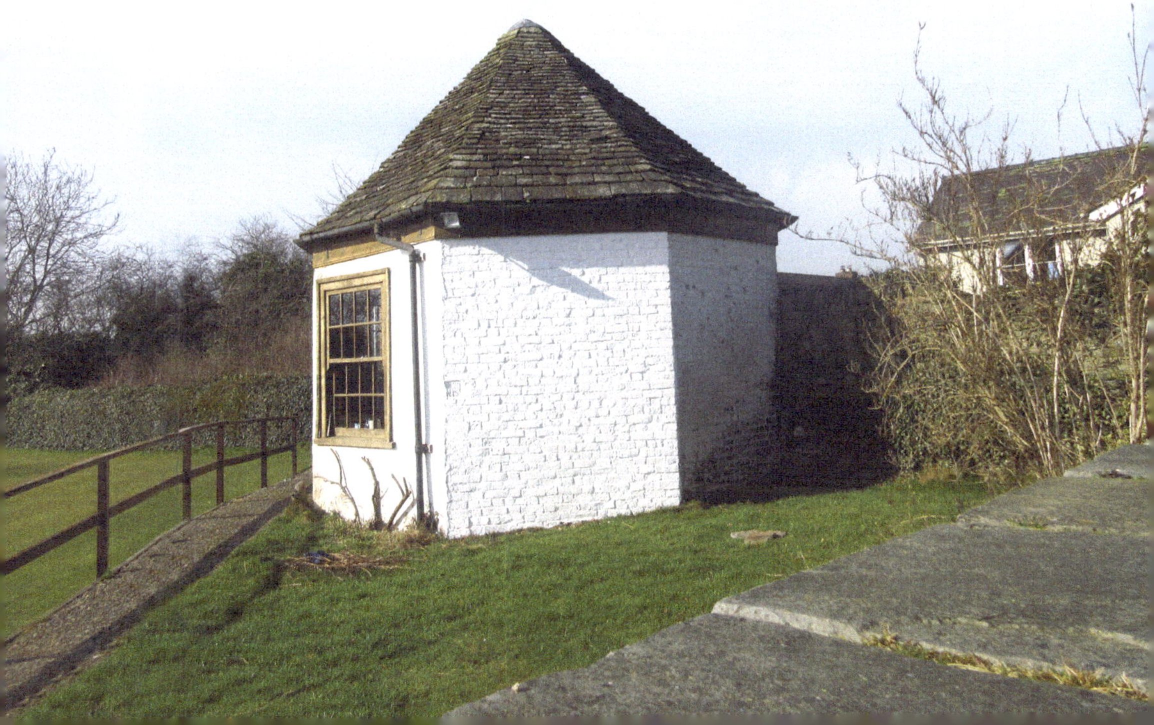

The octagonal clubhouse at Bishop's Castle.

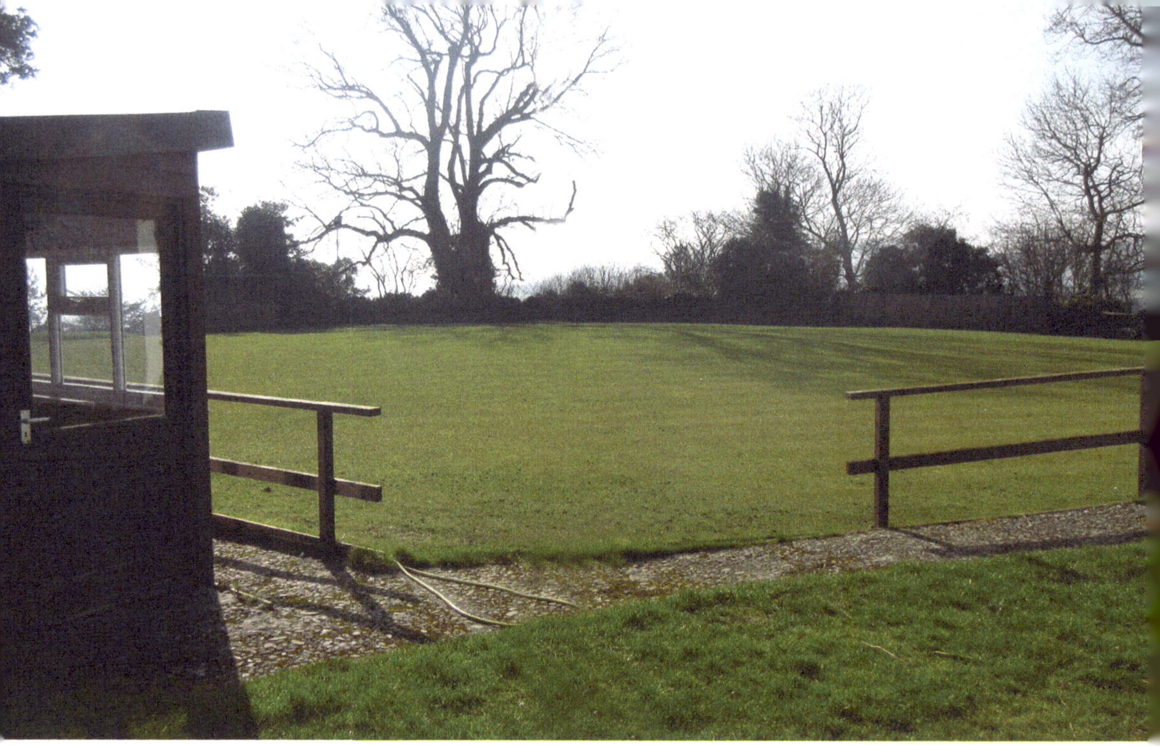

The unique octagonal bowling green at Bishop's Castle.

Records reveal that

> in the Castle they found 13 beeves, 2 waggons, 2 carts, and one white mare. They also found 32 horse loads of wheat, which the Lord Bishop sent thither, and all the produce of one year from two plough lands, in the barn, and the crop of the second year ready to cut, upon the land. There was of armour, six hauberts, one of them without a head, six skull caps of iron, one pair of housings, and an iron surcoat belonging to the Bishop, six cross bows, sound and good, with bandrecks and a tierce quarrels, and the constable's horse. The damage aforesaid destroyed at the Castle and Lydbury, and of timber that lay at the back of the Castle, is valued at 200 marks. Also, the destruction of woods is valued at 100 marks, and the issue of the manor for six years, excepting six weeks, during which the Castle and manor were in the hands of John Fitz Alan, is valued at 360 marks.

During his diocesan visitation in May 1290, Bishop Swinfield spent four nights at the castle. Although there was a weekly market held in the local town, the bishop's baker, who had gone on ahead, found few foodstuffs to purchase there and bought most of the necessary provisions at Ludlow. He'd also taken the precaution of bringing with him his own yeast and salt.

The bishop's accompanying entourage was large, which, just to transport the party and the provisions, required between thirty-forty horses. That number might not seem so large when the provisions that were necessary are taken into account:

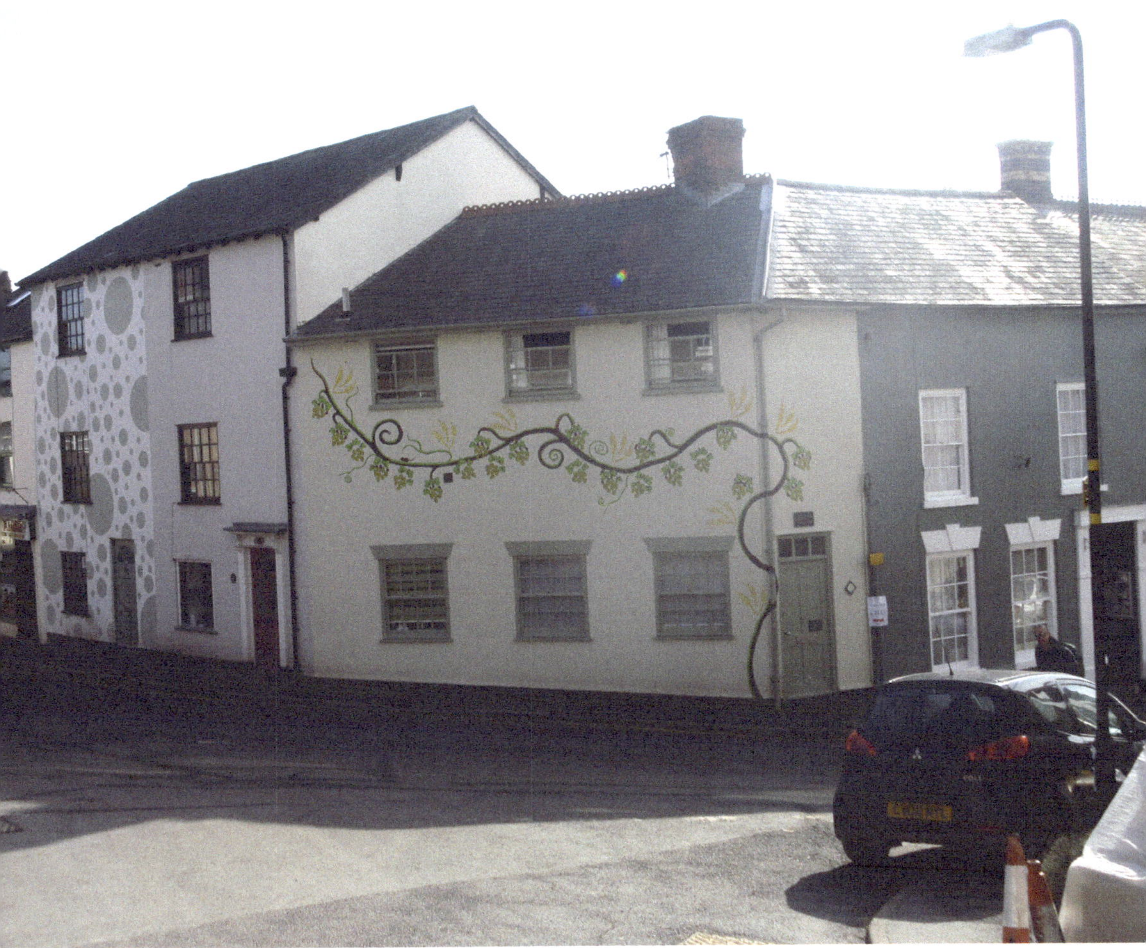

Colourful buildings in Bishop's Castle.

2 quarters of flour, baked from flour brought from the Manor, *6s 8d*;
Beer, 16*d*;
1 carcass of beef cost 6*s* l½*d*;
1 roe, 11 kids, and 2 bacons from the Manor;
2 calves, 12*d*;
13 geese, 4*d*;
3 fowls, 12*d*;
28 capons,
12 fowls a present;
Eggs, lo½*d*;
Milk, 3½*d*;
Bread, 3*d*;
Charcoal, 3*d*.

The above is an extract taken from Bishop Swinfield's Roll of Household Expenses.

Location: SY9 5BN

Boscobel House and the Royal Oak

There is a degree of uncertainty regarding the date when Boscobel House was built, but it is generally acknowledged that it was sometime around 1632. At that time a wealthy landowner, John Giffard of White Ladies Priory, converted a timber-framed farmhouse into a hunting lodge. In need of a name for the new lodge, Giffard called it 'Boscobel House' as it was surrounded by dense woodlands, and the Italian phrase 'bosco bello' means 'in the midst of fair woods'.

John Giffard's family were recusants – Catholics who did not accept the teachings and practices of the established Church of England and refused to participate in their form of worship. This often meant fines, discrimination and, on occasions, imprisonment – for Catholic priests it often meant execution. Because of this, the Giffard family ensured that they surrounded themselves

Sketch of Boscobel House.

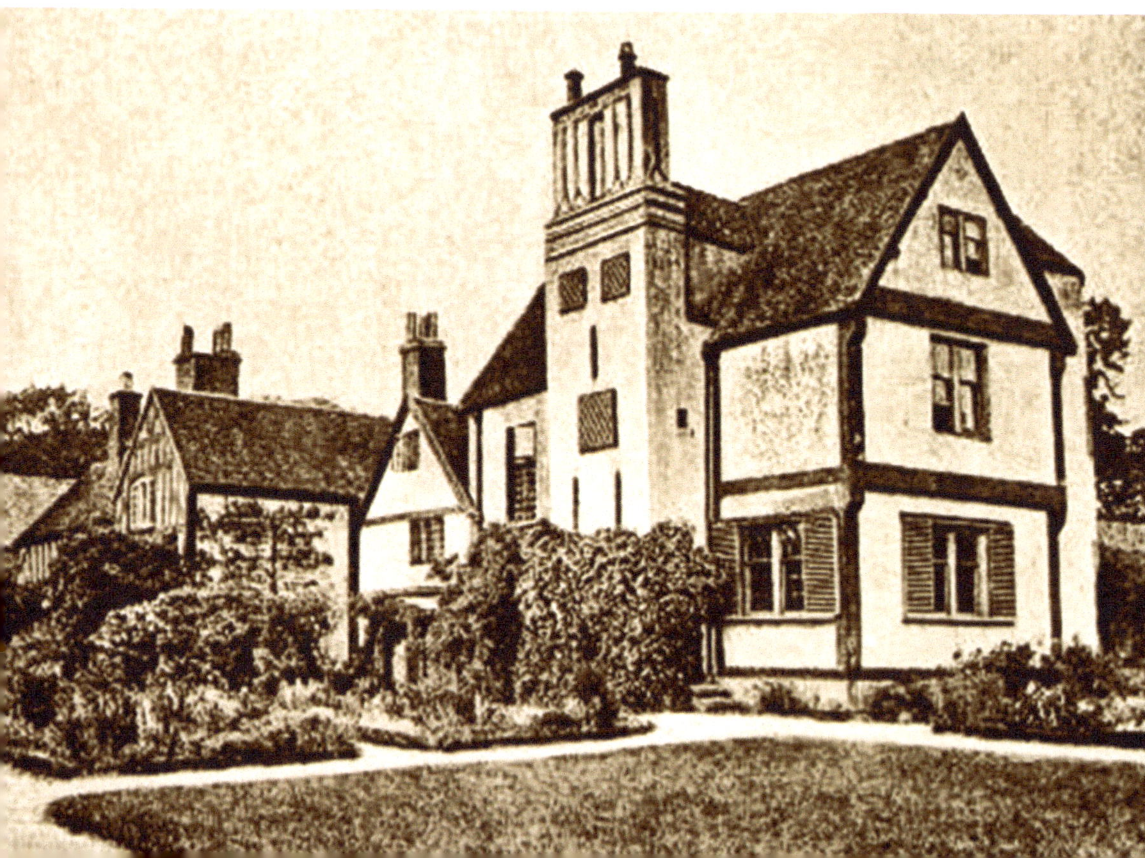

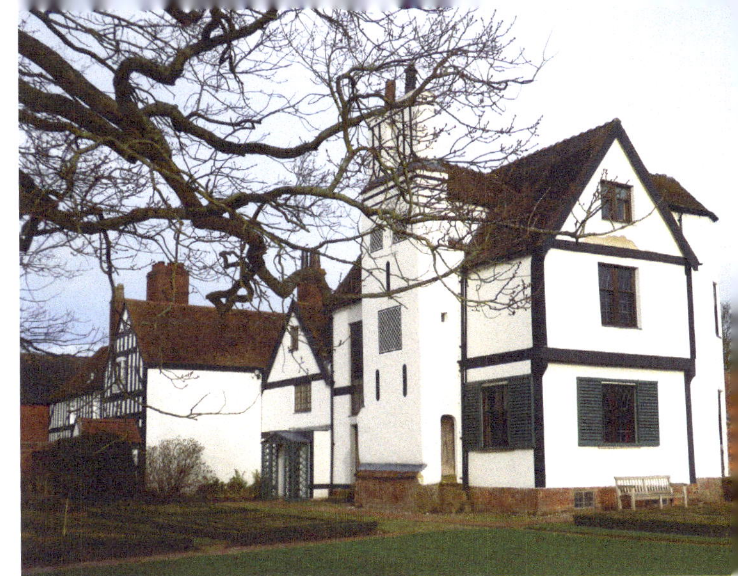

Right: Boscobel House today.

Below: Sketch of White Ladies Priory.

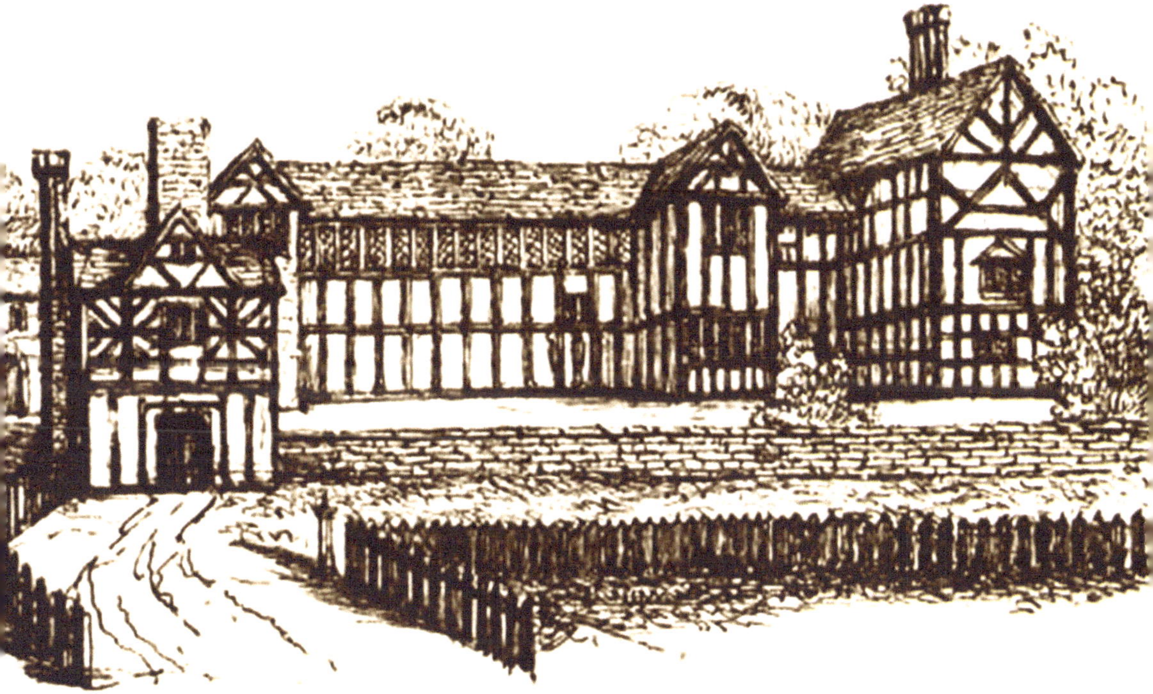

with trusted Catholic retainers. Being situated in dense woods, Boscobel House was often used as a secret place to shelter Catholic priests, having a number of suitable secret places and also several priest's holes. In 1651, when Boscobel gave sanctuary to Charles II, the house was owned by Giffard's heir: his daughter, Frances Cotton.

Directly following the defeat at the Battle of Worcester on 3 September 1651, Charles II was forced to flee for his life. He was taken to White Ladies

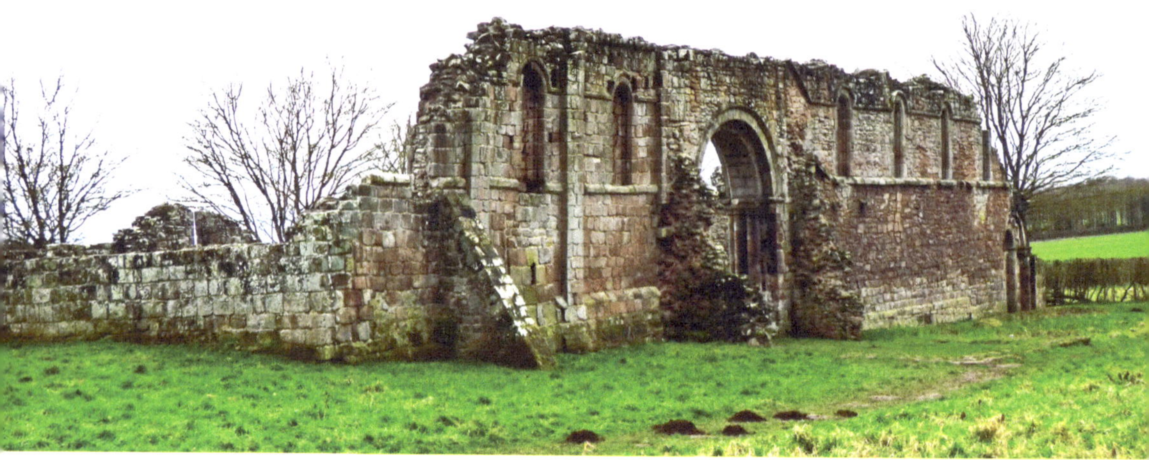

Ruins of White Ladies Priory.

Priory by Charles Giffard, a cousin of the owner. Francis Yates, one of Giffard's servants, was in attendance; subsequently he was the only man to be executed for his part in the escape. Also at White Ladies the Penderel family, tenants and servants of the Giffard family, played an important role in caring for the king. On leaving White Ladies, Richard Penderel attempted to take Charles across the River Severn near Madeley, but was unsuccessful. Forced to retrace their steps, they took refuge at Boscobel, where they were met by Colonel William Careless. However, before entering Boscobel, Careless and the king were forced to spend all day hiding in a nearby oak tree – which later became known as the Royal Oak – as Cromwell's troops in the immediate area had been ordered to scour the area and find the fleeing king. Later, in relative safety, Charles spent the night hiding in the security of a priest's hole in the attic of Boscobel House. From Boscobel the king was taken to Moseley Old Hall, and ultimately, after six weeks of evading capture, Charles managed to flee England in disguise, posing as the servant of Jane Lane of Bentley. At the time there was a £1,000 reward on the king's head and the prospect of death for anyone caught helping him; yet despite this, Charles II landed in Normandy on 16 October 1651.

When Cromwell died in 1658, the stage was set for Charles to return from exile in 1660.

Location: Boscobel House ST19 9AR, White Ladies Priory WV8 1QZ

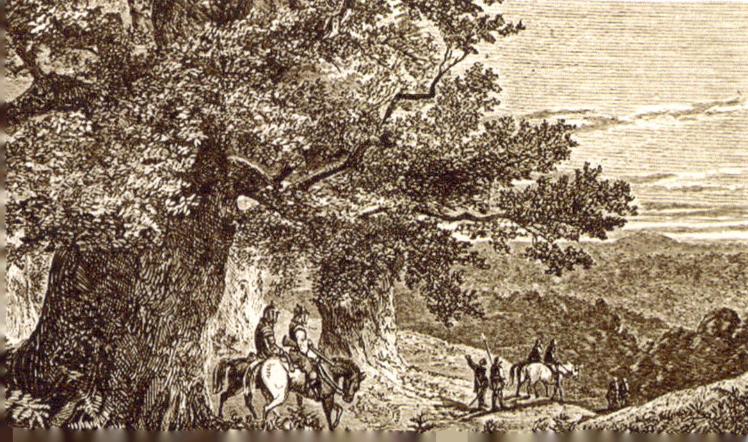

King Charles and Careless hiding in oak.

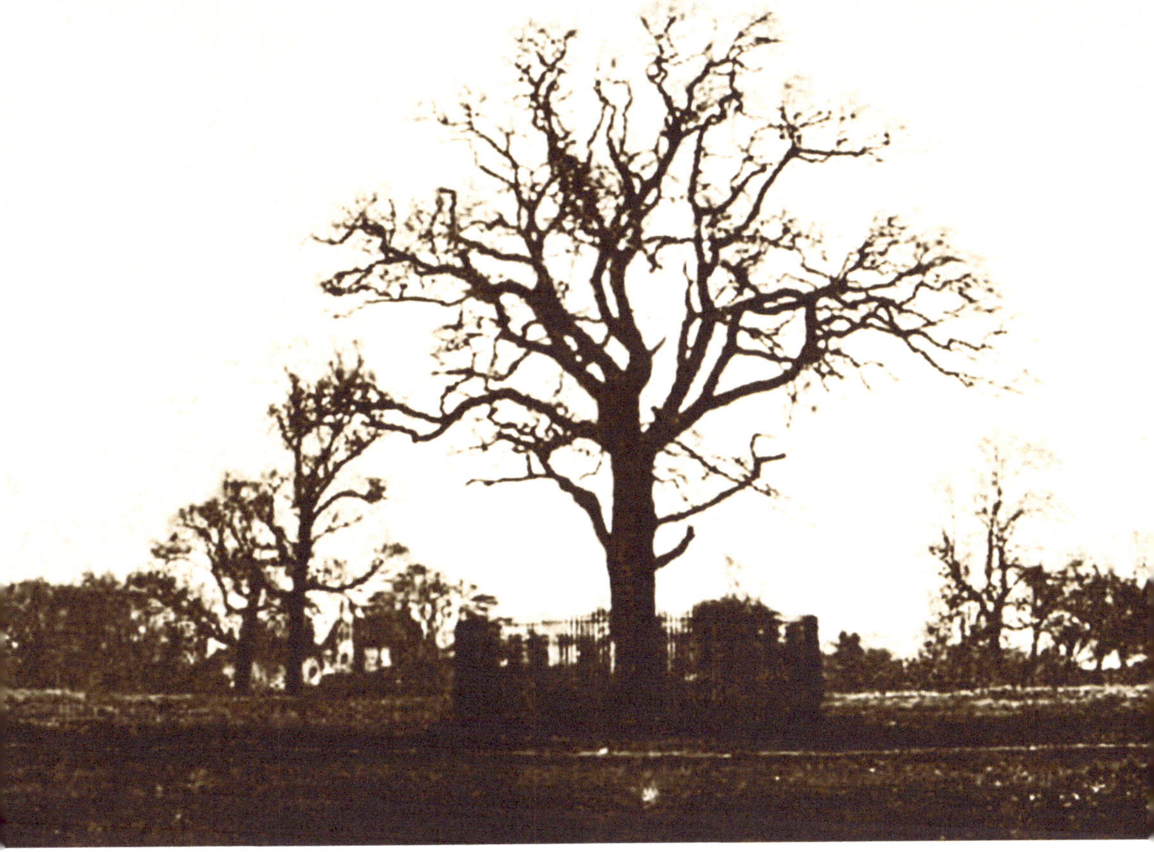

Above: The Royal Oak in 1894.

Right: The Royal Oak today.

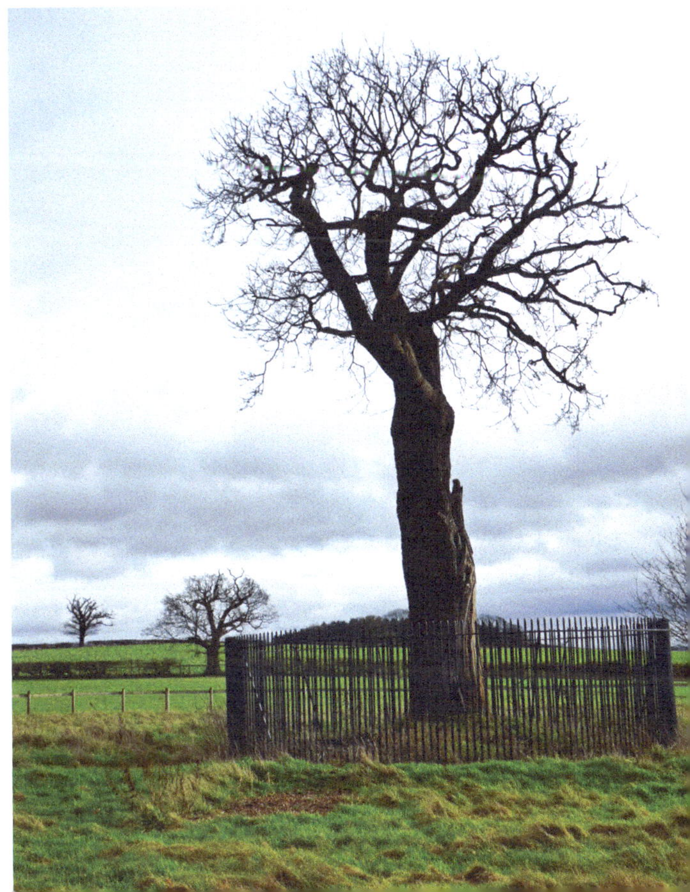

Select Bibliography

Apperley, Charles James (Nimrod), *Memoirs of the Life of the Late John Mytton* (Kegan Paul, Trench, Trubner & Co. Ltd, London, 1835)

Auden, Thomas, *Memorials of Old Shropshire* (Bemrose & Sons Ltd, London, 1906)

Auden, Thomas, *Shrewsbury, A Historical and Topographical Account of the Town* (Methuen & Co., London, 1905)

Acton, Frances Stackhouse, *The Castles and Old Mansions of Shropshire* (Leake and Evans, Shrewsbury, 1868)

Baker, Oliver, *Ludlow Town and Neighbourhood* (G Woolley, Ludlow, 1906)

Blount, Tho., *Boscobel: or, the History of His Sacred Majesties Most Miraculous Preservation* (Henry Seile, London, 1660)

Burne, Charlotte Sophia, *Shropshire Folk-Lore: A Sheaf of Gleanings* (Trübner & Co., London, 1883)

Calvert, Frederick, *Picturesque Views of Shropshire* (William Emans, Birmingham, 1831)

Cathrall, William, *The History of Oswestry* (George Lewis, Oswestry, 1855)

Eyton, Revd R. W., *Antiquities of Shropshire* (John Russell Smith, London, 1859)

Forrest, H. E., *The Old Houses of Shrewsbury* (Wilding & Son Ltd, Shrewsbury, 1911)

Gales, R. L., *The Vanished Country Folk* (Simpkin, Marshall, Hamilton, Kent & Co. Ltd, London, 1914)

Garbet, Revd Sam, *The History of Wem* (G. Franklin, Wem, 1818)

Gaskell, Lady Catherine Milnes, *Old Shropshire Life* (John Lane: The Bodley Head, London, 1904)

Gregory Smith, Revd Canon I., *The Rise of Christian Monasticism* (A. D. Innes & Co., London)

Hartland, Edwin Sidney, *English Fairy and Other Folk Tales* (The Walter Scott Publishing Co. Ltd, London)

Leach, Francis, *The County Seats of Shropshire* (Eddowes's Shrewsbury Journal, Shrewsbury, 1891)

O'Donnell, Elliott, *Haunted Churches* (Quality Press Ltd, London, 1939)

Owen, H., *A History of Shrewsbury* (Harding, Lepard & Co., London, 1825)

Randall, John, *Broseley and Its Surroundings* (The Salopian and West-Midland Journal, Madeley, 1879)

Ritson, Joseph, *English Fairy Tales, Folklore and Legends* (Gibbings & Co. Ltd, London, 1904)

Timmins, H. Thornhill, *Nooks and Corners of Shropshire* (Elliot Stock, London, 1899)

Ward, Andrew H., *A History of the Town of Shrewsbury* (Rogers and Griffin, Worcester, 1826)
Wright, Thomas, *The History and Antiquities of the Town of Ludlow* (Procter and Jones, Ludlow, 1826)
Wright, Thomas, *The History of Ludlow and Its Neighbourhood* (R. Jones, Ludlow, 1852)

About the Author

David Paul was born and brought up in Liverpool. Before entering the teaching profession David served as an apprentice marine engineer with the Pacific Steam Navigation Company. Since retiring, David has written a number of books on different aspects of the history of Cheshire, Lancashire, Yorkshire, Derbyshire, Shropshire and Liverpool.

Also by David Paul:
Eyam: Plague Village
Historic Streets of Liverpool
Illustrated Tales of Cheshire
Illustrated Tales of Yorkshire
Illustrated Tales of Lancashire
Speke to Me
Around Speke Through Time
Woolton Through Time
Anfield Voices

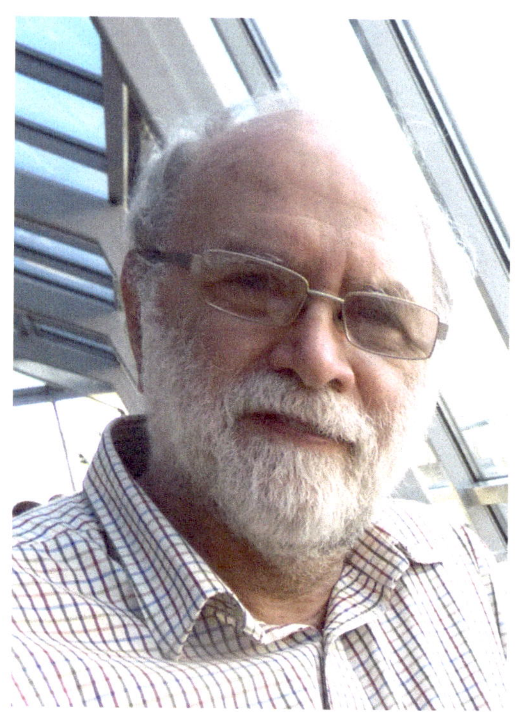

Printed and bound by CPI Group (UK) Ltd, Croydon, CR0 4YY

16/07/2026

02169566-0012